MW01028428

THE WALTER LYNWOOD FLEMING LECTURES
IN SOUTHERN HISTORY

Louisiana State University

Civil War in the Making

1815-1860

BY AVERY O. CRAVEN

Louisiana State University Press

Baton Rouge and London

To Fay Nixon Speer,

a great and inspiring teacher

ISBN 0-8071-0415-9 (cloth)
ISBN 0-8071-0131-1 (paper)
Library of Congress Catalog Card Number 59-7943
Copyright © 1959 by Louisiana State University Press
All rights reserved
Manufactured in the United States of America
1986 printing

Preface

THE ACCEPTANCE of an invitation to deliver a second series of Walter Lynwood Fleming lectures after a lapse of twenty years involves a serious risk. No historian is ever permitted to grow or to change his mind. An opinion once expressed, even in public lectures where generalizations are inevitable, must be lived with as a permanent conclusion for the rest of his life. He is not even allowed to be the authority on why he has written something or what he intended to say. That privilege belongs to those who, regardless of their qualifications, write about " historiography." This being the case, the lecturer who has never read his previous lectures, and hasn't the slightest intention of doing so, runs the serious risk of committing the unpardonable historical sin of being inconsistent.

And what doubles the risk is the fact that this writer happens to entertain a deep suspicion that " historical truth " is a very elusive thing. Viewed from different angles, at different times, for different purposes, even well established facts sometimes take on strange new meanings. Twenty years of continued research and study, and the reading of works by such scholars as James Malin, Roy Nichols, Allan Nevins, David Potter, Fletcher Green, and James Randall, consciously and unconsciously have had their effect. One may still hold to his " honestly-arrived-at " conclusions and yet incorporate whatever does not conflict with his own findings. The result might wrongly appear to indicate a complete change of opinion. That would be an even greater historical crime.

Regardless of the risks involved I have chosen in these chapters to stress interpretation rather than to seek safety in simple narrative. I have always been struck by the intensity of the feelings generated against slavery and slaveholders in men who had no direct or first-hand contact with either. It is conceivable, of course, that they reacted solely to an abstraction which deeply offended their sensibilities and moral values. Yet there was much about their actions and reactions which suggested something more real and personal. I have, therefore, turned to their own environment and experiences in the hope of finding some clue. I have suggested the possibility that behind the determination to put slavery on the road to ultimate extinction there may have lain drives that had little to do with Negro slavery or the American South, as well as others that were the direct product of slavery itself and of the so-called " Slave Power."

More and more I have become convinced that the great body of Americans in 1860 were moderate and conservative in their attitudes; that they came to the brink of Civil War reluctantly. If the term " fire-eater " must be applied it should, I think, be equally distributed between Northerners and Southerners, and it should not be allowed to hide the fact that the great majorities, North and South, were not of this breed.

Lastly I have thought that it might be helpful to understand a very complex past by the use of present-day terms. I have tried to show how absurd it is for historians to argue over the question as to whether the war could have been avoided. Of course it could, that is, *if* things had not gotten into the shape they did, and *if* men had been willing or able to pay the price required for maintaining the peace. Some things, however, are priceless. I have also tried to say that those who can think only in terms of abstractions and legalities (right and rights) had better prepare to use force in the end. There seems to be no other alternative.

My thanks again to Professor Edwin A. Davis of the History Department of Louisiana State University and to the Press of that institution for its efficiency; a growing thankfulness for Bernie, Don, E. B., Al, Walter and all the rest who, without knowing it, have helped. For scholarly criticisms I owe much to Professor Daniel Boorstin.

AVERY CRAVEN

Dune Acres, 1958

vii

Contents

Introduction

ONE HUNDRED YEARS ago the American people were living in an atmosphere of tension, suspicion, and fear produced by a power struggle between two competing ideologies. It was a situation that had grown up during the past decade or more and had become so much a part of men's lives that they accepted it as almost a normal condition. Now and then some unusual development deepened their apprehensions, but, by 1858, they were going about their everyday affairs with little realization that they were on the brink of the passage from a cold war to open conflict.

True, in the Congress, where their representatives met and personalities clashed and harsh words were passed, there had been a rapid degeneration of understanding and co-operation. Newspaper editors in both sections had added something to the situation by reporting only the unpleasant things said and done, but on the whole the life of most common men moved along complacently in accustomed ways so that they were only slightly conscious of the fact that emotions and grievances were piling up to the point where drifting was no longer possible, and where some event would overtopple the accumulation.

Then to make matters worse, just exactly one hundred years ago an economic recession set in to contribute a strange setting for events and to add a part to men's already uncertain attitudes. A few farsighted individuals, sensing the danger, began to talk of a summit conference to face and settle all differences, but that move was delayed until too late, and when the conference did meet in Washington, war was already at hand.

Now history may or may not have lessons to teach the present. I would not care to argue the matter. But I am certain that the present is the only point from which we can view the past. That is why I have chosen the theme about which these chapters turn.

Civil War in the Making

There is more moral and intellectual worth [in the Republican party] than was ever embodied in any political organization in any land . . . . It was created by no man or set of men but brought into being by Almighty God Himself . . . and endowed by the Creator with all political power and every office under heaven . . . .

—HENRY WILSON

This diversity at this moment is appearing not in the forms of denominational polemics, but in shapes as bloody and terrible as religion has ever assumed since Christ came to earth. Its representative, the Church, has bared her arm for the conflict—her sword is already flashing in the glare of the torch of fanaticism—and the history of the world tells us that when that sword cleaves asunder, no human surgery can heal the wound. There is not one Christian slaveholder here, no matter how near he may be to his meek and lowly master, who does not feel in his heart that from the point of that sword is now dripping the last drop of sympathy which bound him to his brethren at the North. With demoniac rage they have set the Lamb of God between their seed and our seed.

—JOHN S. PRESTON to the Virginia Convention

I: The Republican Party and Slavery

THE ELECTION of Abraham Lincoln as President of the United States in 1860 precipitated the secession movement in the Southern states. With South Carolina leading the way, ten other states seemingly reached the conclusion that further connection with the North meant the destruction of their existing social-economic order. They viewed it as a case of submission or secession.

Yet historians agree that Abraham Lincoln was a man of moderate, "old Henry-Clay-Whig" views, who had on various occasions gone out of his way to assure the Southern people that he would in no way interfere with their existing institutions. He had stated bluntly that, were he given all power, he would not know what to do about slavery. Even Alexander H. Stephens had said that Lincoln was "just as good, safe and sound a man as Mr. Buchanan, and would administer the government as far as he . . . [was] individually concerned, just as safely for the South and as honestly and faithfully in every particular." Historians have further noted that, with the Congress and Courts "opposed to him and his principles,"

Lincoln would have been powerless to do harm: that business men were everywhere against further sectional strife; and that the Abolitionists viewed the Republican party as " temporizing," " compromising," and " unworthy of being trusted with [antislavery] interests." Professor Arthur Cole has even accused the secessionists of being moved by abstractions, not realities. " The most thoroughgoing champion of Southern rights," he says, " seldom even hinted that they saw specific dangers looming over the horizon."

With these facts in mind, one may reasonably ask whether Southern fears were justified and whether secession was a rational move. Were Southern social-economic institutions actually threatened? Was slavery in danger? Or had men's emotions just run away with reason and their leadership proven inadequate?

The answers which historians have given to these questions vary widely. James Ford Rhodes and Charles Francis Adams both say that " the alleged grievances of the South [were] mere abstractions." Both talk of repeated Northern " submissions " to the " arrogant " demands of the South. Professor Cole thinks, as did the late Charles Sydnor, that Southern action was the product of an " inferiority complex." The section had become a permanent minority and its sensitive pride in " grasping for ' defensive mechanisms ' preferred ' sublimated ab-

4

stractions ' to realities." Professor Allan Nevins seems
to imply that the South was tricked into hasty action
by its leaders. As he puts it, " the heavy responsibility
for the failure of America in this period rests with
the Southern leadership which lacked imagination,
ability, and courage." Professor Roy Nichols merely
says that " southerners, in a state of hyperemotion,
moved by pride, self-interest, a sense of honor and
fear, rushed to action: they were numerous enough
and effective enough to force secession."

With attention fixed on events as they developed
in secession days, there is evidence to support each
or all of these views. The proud Southerner had un-
doubtedly become oversensitive as he saw his section
become a permanent minority. His sectional leadership was, indeed, as futile in giving sound direction
as was that of the North. Yet can the matter of
Southern fears and action be judged simply by the
immediate situation? Did men act only because of
Lincoln's election, or must we seek the real reason for
Southern reactions through a clearer understanding
of the region in which the Republican party itself
was born and to which it made its appeal?

Southern reaction to Lincoln's election does, indeed, make little sense unless we understand the
simple fact that the Republican victory meant Northern indorsement of certain attitudes basic in Republican thought and the increase of power to give con-

crete expression to them. And since the slaveholder and the institution of slavery played so large a part in the weakening of the old parties and in the creation of new ones, a brief look at some of the implicit assumptions long made in the region where the Republican party flourished, and at recent developments which had again brought these assumptions to the surface, may help us with our problem. The region to be considered stretches from New England to Pennsylvania and spreads across upper New York and westward along the Great Lakes; the period of time is from 1815 onward. The attitudes to be noticed have to do largely with *wealth, its creation and just distribution*; and with *sin and its eradication*.

In the year 1815 a new era opened for the whole western world of which the United States was a part. The almost continuous state of war, which had involved all the nations of Europe for centuries, and which had embroiled the American people throughout colonial and early national days, came to a sudden end. For the next hundred years there would be peace. True, there would be local struggles, but no more world-wide wars. Three generations of fortunate men who lived about the Atlantic Basin could center their thoughts and efforts, undisturbed, on peaceful endeavors.

The matchless age which now began was char-

6

acterized by the rapid accumulation and use of capital for economic ends; by a revolutionary technical advance based on the perfecting of the steam engine for industry and communication; by the intensification of national feelings and activities; and by the spread of a deep democratic-humanitarian impulse. The fusing and maturing of these factors produced what we have called the Modern World.

For the United States as a whole, the century of peace gave the first opportunity to turn away from Europe, to exploit the vast, undeveloped riches of one of earth's richest continents, and to adjust our institutions and our social-economic ways and values to the needs of the age and to those of our continent. For the American South, it meant the rise of the Cotton Kingdom but no great repudiation of existing institutions and values. For the region in which the Republican party was to have its hold, it meant a series of changes, revolutionary in degree, that left few institutions, relationships, or values untouched.

Within little more than the life-span of a single generation, a belt stretching from Massachusetts to Pennsylvania was remade in physical appearance, in its social arrangements, its economic interests, and in the values its people held. Men's bodies were being pushed pell-mell into the modern world of finance-industrial capitalism, while their minds were left

7

behind to struggle with the problems of adjusting the old to the new.

In that struggle every existing institution, every old relationship and value was forced to answer as to fitness for service in the new day. Every new development was asked to measure its merits against old tacit assumptions. A strange, new "hospitality to ideas" went with these demands, and men and women set about with feverish haste to make realities conform to ideals. This was particularly true where new wealth, created by new methods, fell into new hands and thereby created new and strange relationships between those who toiled and those who accumulated.

Work, whether among the Puritans of Massachusetts or the Quakers of Pennsylvania, had always had the dignity of "a calling." "God," wrote a Puritan divine, "doth call every man and woman to serve him in some particular employment . . . . The great governor of the world hath appointed every man his proper post and province . . . and let him be ever so active out of his sphere, he will be at a great loss if he do not mend his own vineyard and keep his own province."

Wealth, in turn, was the product of hard work at one's calling, of thrift, moderation, sobriety and foresight. It was a trust. It was to be gained and used, not for greater self-indulgence, but for the Glory of

8

God. "If God show you a way in which you may lawfully get more than in another way . . . and you refuse this," wrote another, "you cross one of the ends of your calling, and you refuse to be God's steward." "Diligence," wrote William Penn, "is [a] virtue and laudable among Men. It is a discrete and understanding Application of one's Self to Business; and avoids the extremes of Idleness and Drudgery." "Frugality," he added, "is a virtue too, . . . the better way to be Rich, for it has less Toil and Temptation. A Penny sav'd is a Penny got . . . ."

Such were the traditional attitudes towards work and wealth in a region where men, as employers and employees, had long stood on equal ground and bargained freely and with respect for each other. They had thus been strangely prepared both to accept enthusiastically the new finance-industrial capitalism as it came rushing forward, and to quarrel bitterly with it. There would be much of confusion and angry strife but men's tacit assumptions would be made clear and their convictions deepened. The addition of Old World idealists, largely to New York, would only increase the difficulties.

For our purposes, the first significant result of the coming of finance-industrial capitalism to this region, in the years between 1815 and 1844, was the rise of a new and powerful group of business leaders, and the creation of a new and uniquely dependent body of workers. In the beginning, they developed with the textile industry. A decline in commerce made capital available and scattered cotton mills about wherever water power could be found. Overexpansion and depression soon weeded out the least efficient and left the textiles largely in the hands of those who had been able to secure the greatest capital and the most efficient management. Profits soared. Successful groups widened their efforts, bought up power sites, built machine shops, laid out and built whole factory towns, speculated in lands, projected canals and railroads, and found use for their surplus capital in banking and insurance.

Enterprising merchants in Boston, New York City, and Philadelphia found equal opportunities for wealth in the revival and expansion of trade and in the decline of competition from the older centers. Families in both these fortunate groups widely intermarried. Their harsh old Calvinistic beliefs gave way to more rational and dignified ones, and their political needs found expression in the conservative doctrines of the Whig party. A new aristocracy of growing wealth and power had come into being.

But industry had done more than produce capitalists. The young folks who came down from the country to work in the mills soon learned that their move meant considerably more than just an escape from fields and kitchens. Long hours at varied tasks in the open air were one thing; the same hours in a poorly ventilated, lint-filled room spent at a single task, was something else. They also learned that bitter competition between factories in periods of depression meant longer hours, more spindles to tend, and reduced wages. To protest or to strike brought lockouts and black lists. The alternatives were to accept or to leave. By 1844 most New England girls had chosen the latter course, and French Canadian and Irish girls had taken their places.

Workers in the great commercial centers fared little better. According to the *Workingman's Advocate*, they were "despised and trampled upon by the drones and minions of fortune." "The capitalists," complained the New York *State Mechanic*, "have taken to bossing all the mechanical trades, while the practical mechanic has become a journeyman, subject to be discharged at every pretended 'miff' of his purse-proud employer." "A monied aristocracy," they said, was hanging over the worker "like a mighty avalanche threatening annihilation to every man who [dared] to question [the capitalists'] right to enslave and oppress the poor and unfortunate." Workers looked "round them upon the princely palaces and gaudy equipages of the rich" who consumed the fruits of the poor man's labor without adding to "the common stock a grain of wheat or a blade of grass." And when the right to organize was denied by the courts, workers solemnly proclaimed that "the freemen of the North are now on a level with the slaves of the South, with no other privilege than laboring, that drones may fatten on your life blood."

Industry had thus produced a situation in regard to *wealth* and *labor* repugnant to every assumption and value on which the existing social-economic order traditionally rested. Here was wealth greater than ever known before—wealth gained not by men as producers but as masters of capital, middle men, investors and speculators; wealth that held the living of the many in its hands, but which had largely lost the sense of stewardship. And here was work that lacked dignity; wages fixed without bargaining; regulation and control in place of the old freedom.

This was a situation which could not, in this region, long go unchallenged by those capable of disinterested thinking. The factory workers did, after a time, complain and strike. The mechanics of Philadelphia and New York organized, as they said, "to ward off . . . those numerous evils which result from an unequal and excessive accumulation of wealth and power into the hands of the few." But as Professor Commons says, this was not "so much the modern alignment of wage-earners against the employer" as it was one "of the poor against the rich, the worker against the owner." The workers, in fact, were only expressing concern over a situation that had already aroused men and women all over the region whose original point of view regarding wealth and work had not been altered. Among them a deep feeling of unrest had grown as the old order lost ground. Their moral indignation had stirred as they saw " *the few* " living in splendor on the wealth produced by the sweat of other men's faces. Something was bitterly wrong in a land that professed both democracy and Christianity.

Savagely they turned on the new rich. Those who had prospered became a symbol of all that was wrong. Their crime was that they had accepted the Modern World and all its ways. They had betrayed their stewardship. " Here wealth is new and mainly in the hands of men who have scrambled for it adroitly," said the Reverend Theodore Parker, ". . . as a class they are narrow, vulgar, and conceited." They were never to be found " on the moral side of any great question." They never asked " what could be done *for* labor, but only what could be done *with* it." He warned that " if powerful men will not write justice with black ink on white paper, ignorant and violent men will write it on the soil in letters of blood, and illuminate their crude legislation with burning castles, palaces and towns."

Most spokesmen assumed, as did Orestes Brownson, that all wealth was produced " by the toil and sweat, skill and industry of the workers." "All wealth," said Samuel Allen, "is the product of labor and belongs of right to him who produces it, yet how small a part of the products of its labor falls to the laboring class! How large a part of it is wasted, and worse than wasted, upon the pride and vanity and voluptuousness of those who produce no wealth, and render society no equivalent for what they consume." The rich were exploiting the laborer, looking "down on him as a vulgar creature," while "they pocketed the proceeds of his labor . . . filled the high places of society, rode in carriages, sat on cushioned seats and feasted their dainty palates on luxuries culled from every clime."

Thus an artificial state of society had been created in which a "race of non-producers, who render no equivalent to society for what they consume . . . constitute a new sort of aristocracy of a more uncompromising character than the feudal, or any landed aristocracy, ever can be."

Sympathy for the workers was equally intense. "There is not a state's prison or house of correction in New England where the hours of labor are so long, the hours for meals so short, and the ventilation so much neglected as in the cotton mills with which I am acquainted," wrote Dr. Josiah C. Curtis in his report to the American Medical Association. "Could any beast of burden bear the duration of toil imposed on the factory operative? " asked one editor, and then added, " How much better is a horse than a woman." "Where is humanity? " asked another. " It is swallowed up in gain—for the almighty dollar; and for this, poor girls are enslaved and kept in a state little better than the machinery, which, when *it* gets out of repair, is taken to the repair shop and restored: but not so the human machinery—that is kept in constant motion until the motive power is brought to a stop, and what of it then? It is laid to one side and new [human] machinery procured." And what became of the girl who was laid aside? The *Daily Democrat* tells us that " while those who reaped the profits " dropped " their heads on cologne scented handkerchiefs in prayer and thanksgiving every Sabbath day," the poor mill-girl came " to Boston to die in a brothel."

Instinctively the word " slavery " came into use and comparisons began to be made. " At the South," wrote one editor, " the master lives in opulence on the labor of his colored slaves, whose stimulation to exertion is too often the driver's lash, but who are almost universally provided with the absolute necessaries of life in all stages of their existence. At the North, the master has a lash more potent than the whipthong to stimulate the energies of his white slaves: *fear of want*." And because the Northern worker did not see his chains, he was none the less a slave. " Instead of simple chains," said this writer, " he wears a net, that hampers every fiber of his body and every faculty of his soul . . . . Instead of bearing a single wrong, he is crushed by a boundless system of iniquity."

Both the Northern and the Southern master, added another, aimed at and accomplished the same end: " Obtaining labor and service without rendering labor and service in return. How can you reckon the one . . . more atrocious than the other." Many, in fact, did not do so. As one man put it: " When capital has gotten thirteen hours of labor daily out of a being it can get nothing more. It would be a very poor speculation in an industrial point of view to own the operatives, for the trouble and expense of providing for times of sickness and old-age would more than counterbalance the difference between the price of wages and the expense of board and clothing. The far greater number of fortunes accumulated by the North in comparison with the South shows that hiring labor is more profitable capital than slave labor." " Wages," added Orestes Brownson, " is a cunning device of the devil for the benefit of the tender conscience, who would retain all the advantages of the slave system, without the expense, trouble and odium of being slaveholders."

Nor did the man who moved out of this industrial belt into the upper Northwest fare any better. The new capitalist, turned speculator, preceded him, engrossed the best lands and held them for a profit. The cause of the settler and that of the workers whom he left behind, were one and the same. He viewed the speculators as " persons . . . disposed to live out of the labors of others " and who had established " a petty aristocracy " which was choking " the tree of Liberty " and causing " her leaves to wither " so that her sons must " endure the scorching rays and blasting influences of the slavery making idol of money tyrants." Farmers too were slaves, for, as George Evans reminded them: " Give me the air a man must breathe, the water he must drink, or the *Land* from which he must draw his subsistence, and you give me the WHOLE MAN. He must obey me, and serve me, or die."

Regardless of the justice or soundness of these attitudes, they were widely held by clergymen, intellectuals, members of the old substantial families, who found no place in the new order, and by the many whose consciences still responded to traditional values. What was happening did not accord either with their notions of democracy or of Christianity. Is it right? they asked. Does it comport with the spirit of free institutions? Is it republican? Is it American? Reacting to their own social-economic conditions, these men were talking about " the worse than useless aristocrats " and " their abused and exploited slaves."

They were saying things "as harsh as truth and as uncompromising as justice." They were appealing to deeply ingrained convictions and laying the foundations for a wider moral crusade.

A second locality in which powerful forces were at work generating attitudes that would play a fateful part in national life lay in the rural belt that stretched out of New England into Vermont and then westward across upper New York and along the Great Lakes into the interior. It was a region primarily of farms and small towns save where the Erie Canal had altered the pattern. Many of its farms, especially in New York, had been purchased from land companies or were being rented from large holders. Wheat, as the great frontier cash crop, had, by 1840, already crossed this region in its steady westward march. It had, at first, brought profits and had built Rochester as a great milling center. But as it moved on into the farther west, it had left disaster in its wake and the necessity constantly to shift crops. Land and market troubles thus always formed a disturbed background on which events moved. The land agents in Albany and the landlords near at hand kept them conscious of the fact that here also the living of the many was in the hands of the few.

But far more important than economic factors in shaping the attitudes of men in this region was the matter of sin. From the days of Jonathan Edwards the revival meeting had followed migrating New Englanders in their westward trek. So constant and intense had been the revival fervor that upper New York had become known as the "Burned-over District." Fed by a flow of young revivalists out of Yale, and as steady a flow of religious literature from societies in the older centers, men and women in this region set about with a frightening earnestness to rid the world of sin and to usher in the millennium. The grim old Calvinistic doctrine of salvation only through election, already sharply altered, was here reduced to a simple matter of individual willingness to repent and believe. Any man "could if he would" be freed of sin. Under the intense emotions stirred, new revelations from Heaven were received and new churches, that were to form a permanent part of American life, were started. Communities were established where sin could not exist, and the exact date when Christ would reappear and the world come to an end was set. Never in all American life had a more powerful moral force been set in motion, or one more potent for good or ill.

The exaggerated concern with the individual soul, however, and belief that all evil resided there, kept this force, for a time, safely away from social reform. During the 1830's, however, this began to change. Hard times and a growing realization that revival

CIVIL WAR IN THE MAKING

methods had not brought the millennium turned
many disillusioned souls in a different direction. They
moved from the effort at general salvation to an attack
on specific evils. The revivalist turned reformer.
Saving society by removing sin from individuals, one
at a time, was too slow a process in this mad changing
age. It might be better to concentrate on certain
larger manifestations. With all the old crusading zeal,
they turned on war, intemperance, injustice to women,
Negro slavery, and a half dozen other social ills. The
growing improvements in communication under steam
widened the scope of their efforts and made organization and propaganda on state and national levels
possible. They turned reforming into a profession—
a profession, however, that was the heir to all the
techniques of the revival.

At first, efforts were scattered among several re-
forms, but gradually antislavery took over. Slavery's
sinfulness was most apparent and those who practiced
it far enough removed to permit the imagination full
play. Working largely through evangelical churches,
long familiar with the revival, young preachers, turned
reformers, lighted " the fires of freedom " across New
York and on into the upper Northwest. But it was
the same old fight against sin. For slavery, they said,
was " always, everywhere and only sin." " Insist prin-
cipally on the SIN OF SLAVERY," were the instructions
given by the American Anti-Slavery Society to its

agents. "Especially stir up ministers and others to the duty of making continual mention of the oppressed slaves in all social and public prayers." A movement that had begun as an effort to eradicate sin and to usher in the millennium in their own immediate neighborhoods was being broadened into one directed mainly at the institutions of a rival section. Yet the method had not changed. As the American Anti-Slavery Society told the great evangelist, Theodore Weld, when he became their agent, their ends were to be accomplished by showing the public that slavery was contrary " to the first principles of religion, morals and humanity," so as " to produce a just public sentiment, which shall appeal both to the conscience and love of character, of our slave-holding fellow-citizens, and convince them that both their duty and their welfare require the immediate abolition of slavery." In other words, *these sinners* were to be convicted of their sins, and then led to repentance and salvation in the good old revival way. Furthermore, the agent's work was to be carried on, not among the slaveholders themselves, but among those churchmen in the upper North who now needed some new emotional moral drive to take the place of the weakening revival movement.

Until the late 1830's and the early 1840's, the drives against wealth acquired by exploiting labor, and against sin as the deterrent of the millennium, were stirred, as we have said, primarily by local conditions, and the evils to be eliminated were those in the immediate surroundings. The appeal for action was based on democratic and Christian sentiments. In fact, many had begun to fuse the two and to think of their purposes as one. "There is fast rising in New England," wrote George Bancroft, the historian, "a moral Democracy, in harmony with Christianity . . . in harmony with the progress of Civilization." "Democracy is practical Christianity," he concluded. Said Samuel Allen: "Christianity was intended by its divine Founder to lend its powerful aid for the relief and enlightenment of the laboring classes . . . and to change the existing political and economic relations of society." "Democracy," said the *Democratic Review*, "is the cause of Humanity . . . . It is the cause of Christianity . . . of which it has been well said that its prevailing spirit of democratic equality among men is its highest fact . . . ." And it was "to a Believer who rejoiced in the light of Locofocoism, as an outward sign of the inner light of Christianity," that the historian of that movement dedicated his book.

The hard times which came with the Panic of 1837 and its long-drawn-out aftermath added another item to the Christian-democratic values. The economic pinch enabled industrial capitalism to prove its superiority and to establish its dominance. It became the symbol of the Modern Age. Thus *progress* in terms of cities, factories, and railroads became a part of the national *manifest destiny* so boisterously demanded. Henceforth, *Christianity, democracy*, and *progress* would go hand in hand in an aggressive drive that would not be considered aggression because it is not aggression to fight sin, to demand a more democratic order, or to encourage progress.

Meanwhile, the bitter debates in Congress over the receiving of antislavery petitions and the use of the mails seemed to indicate that the real danger to democracy, Christianity, and progress was to be found, not at home, but in a rising slave power. Looking about with an eye long trained to detect sinners, they began to shift the blame for what had happened to them and to the old America, to the aristocrats who lived below the Mason-Dixon line in idle luxury on the toil of abused and exploited slaves; whose sinful ways ranged all up and down the list against which their moral crusades had already been launched. The South had expanded with cotton, but it had not altered its ways or values. It was out of step with progress. It was holding back the rest of the nation, and the agricultural disaster that had overtaken the once prosperous wheat farmers of New England and upper New York was the work of the slaveholder.

Antislavery groups therefore resolved "That the existence of slavery is the grand cause of the pecuniary

23

embarrassments of the country; that no real or permanent relief is to be expected by the establishment of a national bank or sub-treasury, until the total abolition of that execrable system." " Slavery must be destroyed," they insisted, " or the agricultural, mechanical, manufacturing and commercial interests of the country must perish." What had happened, as Elizur Wright said, was that " the industrious North had trusted the slack-twisted financial honor of the South, and it failed." Joshua Leavitt went even further. His explanation was that " The system of society in a slaveholding community is such as to lead to the contraction of debt, which the system itself does not furnish the means of paying . . . ." Masters were extravagant; the slaves wasteful. So debts mounted and " the sense of obligation to pay [was] essentially different between people who always live on the earnings of the poor, and those who have nothing but what they have earned by their own industry." The South by its failure to meet its obligations had taken from the North in the past five years at least $100 million " in notes which will never be paid." So " there was hardly a remote hamlet in the free States that has not been directly or indirectly drained of its available capital by the Southern debt." " Slavery," he concluded, " has been the prime cause of all the financial tornadoes which have swept over our country . . . . It is a bottomless gulf of extravagance and thriftlessness."

That this situation called for political effort was perfectly clear to anyone who observed the way in which the Democratic party, under slave control, " busied itself perpetually with expedients to enhance the price of the products of slave labor, and to open markets to them in all parts of the known world, while it studiously avoided doing anything to procure a market for the free products of the grain growing Northwest." Wheat had lain unharvested for years in the fields of upper New York, yet the slave-controlled government had nothing to remove " the iniquitous corn laws of Great Britain."

The answer came from a convention assembled in November, 1839, at Warsaw in upper New York, when the " Friends of Abolition " resolved " that every consideration of slavery . . . serves only to convince our minds that it involves all the worst features of the vilest sin which can be committed either by individuals or nations." With an appeal to all " Christian freemen " for support, they launched the so-called Liberty party with James G. Birney, of New York, as their candidate for President, and Francis J. Lemoyne, of Pennsylvania, for Vice-President. Soon afterward, their candidate for the presidency declared that the country was in the hands of the slave power; that the North in relation to the South " is a conquered province . . . ." It was vain, he said, " to think of a sincere union between the North and the South, if the first remain true to her republican principles and habits . . . . They can no more be welded into one body . . . than clay and brass." Then, having delivered himself of these sentiments, he departed for England, bearing with him a trunk filled with petitions from upper New York asking for the repeal of the English corn laws.

The Liberty party itself did not play an important role in American political life. It never attracted a large following or gained a decisive vote. But it did reveal a drift in thought and action of profound significance. Here was the first national third party and it carried into the political arena those powerful moral drives against sin and undeserved wealth which lay close to the surface in the thinking of thousands who still clung hesitatingly to the trouble-torn old parties. It centered these drives on slavery as the fundamental cause of national disaster and disgrace. As its leader said: " Where half of a government live by their own work and pay as they go, and the other half, by others' work and by the longest possible credit, and where those halves are made by *climate*— a mighty pecuniary convulsion *must* . . . hurl those two systems of labor and living into mortal conflict, and *must* demolish the basis of all existing parties and recast them in the mould of necessity upon the all controlling principle . . . of *self preservation.*" He was only saying, well ahead of Mr. Lincoln, that this nation cannot endure half free and half slave.

His party had increased and added a new moral force to that turmoil in New York state which would soon hopelessly split the Democratic party and force the Whig party, under William W. Seward, to an antislavery, higher-law position and to its ultimate destruction. It created the fiction that the Democratic party, even before the Mexican War and expansion troubles, was the tool of an aggressive slave power. It fostered the idea that slavery alone determined every Southern, and therefore, every Democratic administration policy. It gave force to the notion that a power struggle, involving " self-preservation," had begun, with additional strength to be added to that antagonist whose social-economic system could be expanded. A cold war was on. As a Southerner asked in 1850: " Is the Union, then, in a wholesome state—is it in a *peaceful* state? Are the people literally at peace, or are they not at war, the worst of wars, a war of words, a war in the dark, at war with swords sheathed, hands tied, and only able to buffet and butt about in the utmost profundity of darkness and corruption . . . . We speak *of facts as they exist.*"

By 1848 the Liberty party was " defunct," not because its appeal had weakened but for exactly the opposite reason. The annexation of Texas, the Mexican War, slavery in the territories and the struggle over the tariff, internal improvements and homesteads, had completely shifted attention from local to national affairs and had so broadened the anti-Southern appeal that it could no longer be confined to a small third party, based on a single idea. Strong factions in both the Whig and Democratic parties were so openly opposed to the spread of slavery and so convinced of slave-power control in government that enlistments for the cold war far outran the capacity of the Liberty organization. Efforts to widen its appeal to include all reform only brought dissension and decline. It disappeared when a new fusion of dissatisfied " Free Democrats," " Conscience Whigs," and disappointed Liberty men launched the Free Soil party.

That party was *new* only in name. It represented primarily the adjustment of old attitudes and assumptions to changed conditions. The atmosphere was still that of the revival; the spirit, that of a crusade against sin. Joshua Leavitt, the old Abolitionist, who arose to make the nomination of ex-President Martin Van Buren unanimous, choked with emotion as he declared: " Mr. Chairman, this is the most solemn experience of my life. I feel as if in the immediate presence of the Divine Spirit." And he was right when he shouted: " The Liberty Party is not dead, but translated." Stripped of the personal motives involved, the Free Soil party merely transferred the moral assumptions held against slavery *per se* to the extension of slavery, and enlarged the charges made against "the slave power" to include opposition to the domestic policies essential to the continued development of the North and West. It played a part in the election of a Whig President, but, more important, it revealed the political chaos that existed in the region and the growing tendency to fight the economic battles under the banner of righteousness.

After this the only step yet to be taken was the one by which men who were convinced that slavery was morally wrong would cease to tolerate it on Constitutional grounds. Charles Sumner had seen their dilemma as early as 1847. Speaking of the Free-Soil Whigs, he said: "They have proclaimed slavery to be *wrong*, and have pledged themselves with force against its *extension*. It is difficult to see how they can longer sustain themselves *merely* on that grounds. Their promise sustains a broader conclusion, that is, the duty of no longer allowing the *continuance* of evil anywhere within our Constitutional action. They must become Abolitionists . . . ."

William H. Seward solved their dilemma. He removed the Constitutional barrier. "I know that there are laws of various sorts which regulate the conduct of men," he said. "There are constitutions and statutes, codes merchantile and codes civil; but when we are legislating for states, especially when we are founding states, all these laws must be brought to the standard of the laws of God, and must be tried by that standard, and must stand or fall by it." There was a higher law than the Constitution.

Meanwhile, Theodore Weld and his band of seventy had given the evangelical Northwest a vivid picture of the brutality and injustice of slavery, culled, they said, " from the testimony of a thousand witnesses." Harriet Beecher Stowe popularized that picture and gave it a vitality which only fiction can bestow. Then, in turn, Democratic Presidents, backed by the votes of Southern men, who, as a Chicago editor said, showed themselves " to be slave-holders, but not Americans," vetoed the legislation that would have given the internal improvements and homesteads so vital to Western development. And to cap the climax, Stephen A. Douglas now seemingly threatened to open the vast territories of Kansas and Nebraska to the further increase of the slave power.

The Republican party which sprang into being all over the North and West in 1854 and triumphed in 1860 was occasioned, but not created, by the Kansas-Nebraska Act. It was a spontaneous reaction to threats which men believed were being made by what they had been calling " the Slave Power." But it was more than that. It was an aggressive assertion of their determination to have the freedom and government aid necessary to develop their social-economic life to fullness, and an implied notion of values as they conceived of them in Christianity and democracy. The Republican party was the final political expression of all the forces, old and new, which had already produced the Liberty and Free Soil movements. It was, however, more mature, more sophisticated, and wider in its makeup and appeal. Into its ranks had come those democratic Democrats who had given a locofoco quality to Van Buren's administration, and had begun an open break with their party in the 1840's. It had absorbed the old Northern Whigs, who under Seward's and Thurlow Weed's skillful leadership had become both democratic and anti-slavery without sacrificing their economic program of tariffs, central banking, internal improvements with federal aid, and their intense belief in a consolidated Union. They had made these all good Republican principles and planted in the party seeds that one day would produce the " Age of Big Business." The Republican party could thus present a neatly balanced program of interests and principles. As a driving force, it could draw both on the moral assumptions of the reformers, the sharp resentments which had been built up against the Democratic party for its neglect of Northern and Western interests, and the

31

demands for progress as required by the Modern Age. Thus, in spite of the fact that thousands had voted the ticket for other reasons, the Republican party as the professed defender of Christianity, democracy and progress was, to many of its members, as much a crusade as it was a political party. But it was a crusade in reverse, because its mission, as its members understood it, was to see that the nation remained true to its great ideals and achieved its manifest destiny.

What this meant to the South, unless it yielded its ways and values, was an existence under relentless attack, waged in a spirit soon expressed in a blood-curdling battle hymn, with millennial overtones, which begins:

> Mine eyes have seen the glory of the Coming of the Lord:
> He is trampling out the vintage where the grapes of wrath are stored;
> He hath loosed the fateful lightning of his terrible swift sword;
> His truth is marching on.

January 2, 1861

. . . *South Carolina reminds me very much of an Old Woman who has been engaging in scoulding all her life until at last she works herself up into a fit of hysteria and has all kinds of fantasies and imaginations & that she must be prepared to fight everybody & like a wild-cat is ready to fly at any person who looks at her . . . . I wish Old Hickory had been in the White House. I think matters would have been differently managed . . . . But I think So. Carolina acted a dastardly & cowardly part in sneaking like a rat out of a falling house—instead of attempting to reform the Government & by remaining in the Union has rendered powerless the party she pretends now to be contending against, by running away & leaving everything in the hands of our enemies . . . .*

The secession or revolution of So. Carolina will be a blot on her history darker than that of the French Revolution, treacherous to her Southern colleagues, foolish & rediculous to herself & the laughing stock of all Europe . . . .

—JA. C. JOHNSTON (Hayes, N. C.)

II: The Conservative Southerner

THE ELECTION of 1860 served notice on the American South that it must, "within a reasonable time," enter the Modern World. It must accept national consolidation, industrial capitalism, and a more democratic social order. The men of the North who had once opposed and criticized most of these things had now accepted them and had transferred their fight against wealth gained by exploiting labor and against sin, to the Southern slaveholder. The South had lost the struggle for equality in the central government. Calhoun had admitted that in 1850. It would henceforward be a permanent minority. It had lost its fight for equality in the territories. California and Kansas had shown that. And now slavery and white supremacy must be set on the road to ultimate extinction.

The South would have to accept what a majority, now residing in the North, called "progress." They would accept it because the entire struggle between North and South had, as Abraham Lincoln told Alexander H. Stephens, now been reduced to the simple question of the right or wrong of slavery. And William H. Seward had made it clear "that slavery must give way, and will give way, to the salutary instructions of economy, and to the ripening influences of humanity; that emancipation is inevitable, and is near; that it may be hastened or hindered; and that whether it shall be peaceful or violent depends on the question whether it be hastened or hindered; that all measures which fortify slavery or extend it, tend to the consummation of violence; all that check its extension and abate its strength, tend to its peaceful extirpation." The conflict was " irrepressible." It was, as Lincoln said, part of " the eternal conflict between truth and error."

Southerners accepted this as the Republican position. As one wrote: " The Republican creed after March 4, 1861, will be the Constitution of the country. Its High Priest presents the South as the sacrifice on its altar, with the poor privilege to choose a slow or a violent death . . . ." " The question before the country," said another, " is the extinction of slavery. No man of common sense, who is not prepared to surrender the institution with the safety and independence of the South, can doubt that the time for action has come—now or never! "

The fact that slavery was an economic institution involving millions of dollars; that it carried with it a race question of enduring proportions; that it had to do with political strength through the three-fifths rule; and that it was a social thread hopelessly woven into the Southern pattern, did not enter into the

Republican assumptions which, though not always stated, implied a program for ultimate achievement. And that program carried no promise of co-operation. It was evidently to be achieved by the traditional course of the sinner merely giving up his sins.

The economic and social threats involved were, to say the least, somewhat staggering. The air of moral superiority and self-righteousness which accompanied them was, perhaps, even a greater force in producing angry and unreasonable reactions. As Judah P. Benjamin said, " it was not so much what the Republicans had done or might do, as the things they said." It was the assumptions made by what he called " that pestiferous breed—the fools and knaves of New England—that the Earth belongs to the Saints and they are the Saints of the Lord," that rankled. Edward B. Bryan could shrug off the material threats, but what made his blood boil was " the untiring efforts which are constantly made by the people of the North to degrade the South in the eyes of all who come within their reach . . . ." They ignored the feelings of slaveholders; denounced " the state of religion "; denied " the piety of ministers "; and " cast odium on the state of morals at the South." They even slandered the Negroes' " character by charges of ingratitude."

How much the harsh denunciation of slavery as a

CIVIL WAR IN THE MAKING

sin and the slaveholder as a sinner, as "a crime, a damning crime," had to do with the creation of extreme attitudes in the South, is difficult to estimate. It must have been considerable. Men could not have been indifferent to the charges openly made that Southern congressmen were " desperadoes "; that " we would sooner trust the honor of the country . . . in the hands of the inmates of our penitentiaries and prisons than in their hands . . . they are the meanest of thieves and the worst of robbers . . . . We do not acknowledge them to be within the pale of Christianity, or republicanism, or humanity." They may have been wrong in saying, in 1860, that the Republican party and the President " have proclaimed hatred, abhorrence, scorn, and loathing of the Southern men and women," but there can be little doubt about the fact that they were angry. Nor did these people show that they were a peculiar breed of human beings when they felt this way. They were simply meeting emotion with emotion. They were not revealing to all the world, as a recent historian implies, that all Southerners were peculiarly militant.

The South, of course, did have citizens who well merited the title of " fire-eaters." Their extreme attitudes and words have been noted and quoted so widely that all other Southerners are nearly forgotten. Yet the number who rightly deserve to be called extremists is not large, and no larger than the number whom Southern neighbors would have called "extreme moderates." Neither group were typical of the great body of Southerners who, in 1860, accepted secession because they could not help themselves.

Like most rural-agricultural peoples the majority of the men and women who lived in the South were orthodox and conservative in their own peculiar way. In religion they agreed with their great preacher, James H. Thornwell, that Christianity had "no commission to construct society afresh, to adjust its elements in different proportion, to rearrange the distribution of its classes, or to change the forms of its political constitutions." Neither he nor they hoped or expected that the world would be converted into a paradise. The business of the Christian was simply to ease the harshness of such things as poverty, sickness, and slavery.

As to democracy, it reached its fullest expression where slaves carried the drudgery of life and thus permitted a high degree of equality among the whites. It worked best where the few with superior ability accepted the obligation to honest, efficient public service. There was no such thing as the absolute equality of all men, so that nowhere except in the slaveholding states was there, as Senator Brown of Mississippi said, " a living, breathing, exemplification of the beautiful sentiment that all men are equal . . . a whole Community standing on a perfect level, and not one of them a tithe of a hair's breadth higher in the social scale than another."

And as to progress, they were content if prosperity continued, and if those who played the game according to accepted rules were able to move forward towards the goals which measured success. That included growth and expansion for the nation as well as for individuals. It did not include an interest in radical change or " isms."

A brief survey of men and events up to 1860 bears out the contention that Southern opinion, like Northern, was generally conservative. There were periods of excitement but on the whole the masses were surprisingly calm. Reactions were as often to Northern attitudes as to events themselves. It was never safe for the more radical spokesman to leave action to the freely expressed will of the masses. Even the vital question of secession was not submitted to the voters.

The Missouri Compromise struggle is often considered to have been the point at which the North-South conflict first broke into the open. Speaking of Southern public opinion at that time, Professor Glover Moore, the historian of the event, says:

> It might be supposed that the introduction of the Tallmadge amendment in February, 1819, and the sulphurous debate that followed would have electrified the

whole South. Instead only the Southern members of Congress were electrified! During the summer of 1819, after the first Missouri debate, Southerners appeared to be blissfully unaware of the fact that they were engaged in a mighty sectional contest. Nowhere was popular indifference more marked than in Charleston, the future citadel of secession . . . . Not until antislavery meetings were called in the free states and Northern legislatures and pamphleteers became active did the South begin to evince anything remotely resembling public interest in the Missouri question.

Even then, outside of Virginia, where motives were highly tangled, indifference remained the dominant attitude. Both the slavery issue and that of state rights were involved in the struggle, but neither, as yet, seemed to carry much of emotional force. The masses were far more concerned with the Panic of 1819 than with abstractions.

The South Carolina nullification episode of 1832 is often viewed as a direct step on the road to secession. Yet, as a matter of fact, with a perfectly justifiable shift in emphasis, it might be viewed as a revelation of growing nationalism. The most interesting thing about Calhoun's *Exposition and Protest* was the studied effort to find a strictly legal or Constitutional method of getting rid of an unsatisfactory law. As a Harvard professor of government has recently said, Calhoun's theory was " a conservative theory " and " In the perspective of the Civil War, the Harpers and McDuffies of 1832 cease to be ' revolutionaries,' cease to be ' jacobins.' They become men of peace, trying to solve by legal means the only problem in American history that has shattered completely the framework of our legal institutions." Calhoun himself bluntly declared that South Carolina was " acting with devoted loyalty to the Union " and that if " civil discord, revolution or disunion " were to result, he would, " at any hazard " step in to " arrest it."

Nor can nullification be considered, in any way, an expression of Southern sectional consciousness. Not another Southern state approved. They disliked the tariff as much as did South Carolina, but nullification as a threat to national supremacy was no remedy. They called it " a mischievous and absurd heresy " (Virginia), a " ridiculous and reckless plan " (Georgia), and insisted that the people of South Carolina were " completely deluded " (North Carolina). Mingled with their rejection of nullification was praise for the Union. " The dissolution of our Union," said the Augusta, Georgia, *Constitutionalist*, " would be one of the heaviest blows ever struck at the happiness of the human race." " The benefits of this Union are inestimable," echoed the Richmond *Enquirer*.

This latter paper, soon to be classed as a " fire-eater," hailed President Jackson's proclamation against South Carolina as "worthy of the patriot who has devoted his best days to the glory of his country and to the liberties of the human race. The patriotism which breathes in this production is entitled to all our gratitude." ". . . To every argument which it urges against the doctrines of South Carolina, we cordially subscribe . . . . We agree thoroughly with the President, that the doctrine of nullification strikes a blow at the Union—that it would scarcely be equal to a rope of sand, if every State had the right to nullify every law which it might pronounce to be contrary to the Constitution . . . ."

Nor did South Carolina herself lack in moderate men. The *Enquirer* rightly spoke of "the struggle" as being one between such extremists as Hamilton, McDuffie, Preston, Turnbull, Barnwell, and Smith, and such moderates as Petigru, Drayton, Poinsett, Huger, Blair and Mitchell. With eyes too intently fixed on 1860, we are inclined to give too much attention to the radicals and to forget that Poinsett and his Charleston friends kept President Jackson well informed as to what steps were best; that men in the western part of the state resolved that they would never "obey any call on her militia to march against the government of the United States," and that they defied "the tyranny of the nullifiers," scorned "their insolence" and despised "their menaces." We have ignored the young editor of a South Carolina newspaper who wrote: "We will advocate and advance, to the best of our abilities, the doctrines professed and acted upon by the Union Party throughout our State. We oppose everything savouring of nullification and Disunion; for we do not believe that any State has a right to nullify an Act of Congress . . . . We do not believe that a State has the right to secede . . . . We do not believe that South Carolina is sovereign . . . ." His name was William Lowndes Yancey.

In the years between 1832 and 1850, changes heavy with threat to the nation's future took place in both North and South.

In the North, the new industrial order reached maturity and was ready to begin the final struggle for national social-economic control. The restless ferment and questioning which the new age had produced now reached the stage of affirmation and centered its force to a large degree on slavery. A war with Mexico, territorial expansion, and a sharp urge towards the realization of " manifest destiny " shifted the emphasis from abolition per se to the denial of slavery's right to expand into the territories. On *this* issue, economics, politics, and morals united in a common drive.

In the South, the Cotton Kingdom also reached a

degree of maturity. Conscious of its strength, sensitive to checks or criticism, it was ready to lend its support in defense of the old Southern interests and values, and to back the demand for equality in national affairs. Its confident spokesmen were in no mood to accept anything less.

The clash of interests and values which, in the late 1840's, turned a political power struggle into a national crisis came with the introduction of the Wilmot Proviso—a move to prohibit the expansion of slavery into that great southwestern empire acquired from Mexico. Unless one accepts the unfounded charge that the annexation of Texas and the Mexican War were proslavery moves "to lug new slave states in," the Proviso must be viewed either as an aggressive move in a power struggle or as a normal step in the antislavery crusade justified by the assumption that slavery was a sin—a national disgrace. It might conceivably be viewed as a combination of the two. In either case, Southerners, with their normal assumptions, were bound to consider the move a deliberate act of aggression against their legal rights. Even moderate men were indignant. They did not consider slavery a sin, and they did not think that the denial of equal access to territory won by "common blood" had anything to do with their morals. They viewed the Wilmot Proviso as a move to weaken their strength in a power struggle, and to deny them equality in national life. The only question in offering resistance was the matter of degree.

First reactions were sharp and angry, whether coming from the Border States or the Deep South, from Whigs or Democrats. The Richmond *Enquirer* expressed an almost universal feeling when it asked: " Do the wicked men of the North imagine that we will be silent or inactive when enactments are proposed incompatible with our existence as freemen? If such be their delusion, the sooner it be removed the better . . . . We again repeat to them that this hitherto blessed Union cannot and will not stand but on principles which guarantee alike both Northern and Southern rights."

Tension increased and passions mounted as the Proviso was reintroduced. The climax was reached with Mississippi's call for a Southern convention and with the harsh debates over Henry Clay's proposals in Congress for adjusting sectional differences. There were constant threats of secession and talk of " the preservation of the Union, if we can, the preservation of our rights if we cannot." Yet the significant thing about the struggle, as far as the South was concerned, was the quick emergence of a clear-cut Union sentiment and a conservative approach.

Interest in the Southern convention weakened rapidly after the first inflamed days. Nashville citizens from the beginning were skeptical of its purposes and others soon began to sense danger. The convention might do something rash, something radical. Soon it became necessary for its supporters to give assurance of its peaceful intentions—that it was, as one editor put it, " just a friendly Southern meeting " called for the purpose of consulting " as to the best means of allaying the agitation which . . . [was] continually imperilling the friendly relations of these States . . . ." Some even went so far as to declare it a meeting to adopt " measures by which the Union [might] be preserved."

Before it ever met, the Southern convention, re-gardless of its badly battered original intentions, was doomed to failure. Only nine states were represented and many of the delegates had no official credentials. Many had come to make sure that nothing extreme was done. In the light of history, the real significance of the Nashville Convention is that it revealed the weakness of dis-Union sentiment in the South and the prevalence of a genuinely conservative outlook.

The Compromise struggle itself, while it brought much bitterness to the surface, showed the same things. Some Southern spokesmen in Congress made violent and threatening speeches. So did some North-ern spokesmen. The number of each is about the same. On the other hand, men from both sections worked for compromise, and credit for its success must be equally divided. But what really turned the tide as far as the South was concerned, was the conservative attitude of the people back home. There were some extremists, of course, especially in South Carolina, but as an editor in a neighboring state put it: " Now we have as little sympathy for the abolition fanatics, and we despise them as heartily as anyone in the world, but we must confess we see no use in such carryings on as our South Carolina friends are indulging in. What good does it do? " " No good," answered another, " only to aid the abolitionists in their desire to break up the Union."

Nowhere outside of the South did those who wished compromise for the sake of the Union, break old political ties. In three Southern states, Georgia, Alabama, and Mississippi, conservatives abandoned old political connections and formed what they significantly called a Union Party. In each case their candidates for state office were elected by a handsome majority. Perhaps, as Herschel Johnson said, ". . . the people of the South [were] not properly awake to the danger—not thoroughly nerved to united resistance," but the fact remains that they " refused to throw up their caps and shout for the dissolution of the Union." As the candidate for governor in Mississippi wrote the governor of South Carolina: " Experience has fully demonstrated that united action cannot be had; the frontier slave states are even now indicating a disposition to cling to the Union at the hazard of their slave institutions."

The last ten years before 1860 held much that would undermine the normal conservative attitudes of Southern people toward national affairs. They accepted the Compromise with repeated threats of serious action in case Northern men should not live up to its provisions. Yet they soon learned that this was an impossibility. The North itself was being thrust forward into the Modern World both in things material and things spiritual. Slavery simply did not belong in the new age either as an economic institution or as a part of its values. Men who already believed that slavery was morally wrong and that slavery alone was responsible for Southern "backwardness" were bound to tolerate those who were determined to do something about it. And they did. So Southerners, in the end, accepted the violated Compromise simply because they were so badly divided among themselves and because they disliked strife and did not wish to renew it.

Realization of the fact that the Compromise had not ended the slavery struggle came with the introduction of the Kansas-Nebraska bill in 1854. Without going into the complicated matter of its origins, it can, at least, be asserted with confidence that it was not the product of a Southern grass-roots movement. Nor did it, at first, stir much interest in the region. As the Richmond *Enquirer* noted in March, 1854, there was "a repugnance to agitation throughout the South" at this time. "We had enough, and too much excitement during the Compromise Controversy of 1850, and now there exists an indisposition to popular meetings and legislative resolves."

Others spoke of the widespread indifference to the bill and contrasted the calm in the South with the fire that was raging in the North. Although the bill left the question of slavery to the people in the territory and declared the Missouri Compromise "inoperative and superseded," few Southerners expected it to result in the expansion of slavery. Certainly the author of the bill did not. Only two of more than fifty Southerners who spoke in Congress voiced such a hope. Southern editors were just as realistic. The great majority in every state thought that climate was against slavery and the more foot-free Northern settlers would early control Kansas for freedom. Many viewed the whole business as an unfortunate renewal of strife. So when the New England Emigrant Aid Company tried to make a race out of settlement, the Southern effort to accept the challenge was a dismal failure. There simply was no genuine interest. The only appeal that seemingly reached any depth was that of defending Southern equality as an abstract right. The only show of emotions came from what the Richmond *Enquirer* called the "unnecessary insult," "the humiliation," "the badge of inferiority and [the] stigma of disgrace," shown in the Northern effort to "superadd the ordinance of man to the decree of God." What was to be done by action was, therefore, left to the Missourians, who had to live next door, and to the politicians in Washington who specialized in talk.

When the final "smoke and dust" had settled, the New Orleans *Daily Crescent* summed up this whole business for the conservative South. The Kansas bill had been an "indiscreet, injudicious and uncalled for measure." It had "asserted a principle that was true, but in its assertion accomplished nothing valuable to the South, while it gave new life to the fanaticism of the North . . . . It had awakened an agitation once allayed, and given new pabulum to an exhausted excitement."

In spite of the fact that the South as a section was to be denounced as never before for unscrupulous aggression in the Kansas affair, the historian must look to the North, not to the South, for extremists. Moreover, whatever contribution Kansas made towards hastening the "irrepressible conflict" must be charged to Northern men.

And that contribution was enormous. Kansas more than anything else enraged the Northwest. All the hatred and distrust that Stephen A. Douglas had accumulated in that region was now turned against the South. All the unrest and bitterness felt towards the Democratic administration for neglect of Northwestern interests was lodged against the slaveholder. All the moral indignation that had been generated in the revivals and the antislavery crusade was now heaped upon the section that was supposed to have treacherously attempted to spread its sinful and retarding institution on to soil dedicated to freedom. To express the whole accumulation of fears and ideals and bitterness, the Republican party spontaneously sprang into being. *That* is the real significance of Kansas.

It was the strength which the Republican party showed in the election of 1856, and the clear understanding of what it threatened, that sealed the fate of the Southern conservatives. They would speak out again on occasion but they had lost their vitality and their ability to stand against the currents of emotion. Throughout the summer of 1856 the Southern press warned the people of the strength and crusading fervor which the Republican party had acquired from the Kansas struggle. " For the first time since the adoption of the Federal Constitution," one wrote, " a Presidential canvass is being conducted on purely geographical grounds. For the first time an important party in the North has arrayed itself under sectional banners and is striving to elevate a man to the Presidency on the one, simple, exclusive, distinct idea of hostility to the South." Reliance on Northern conservatives to put down fanaticism had failed. The old assurance "that the abolition party of the North was . . . a faction equally without respectability and destitute of power" had proven worthless.

"Every year has developed the encroachments of this fanaticism upon the domains of common sense and common honesty," wrote one editor, "until now the waters cover the whole surface of society . . . . Are we longer then to have our vigilance charmed away," he asked, "by the loud professions of the power of a party to defend us which is utterly impotent to protect itself? . . . It is weakness and childish folly to talk longer of any hope outside ourselves . . . . We must meet the foe. We must conquer a peace. In the Union if it may be, but peace we must have." Most agreed that should John C. Frémont be elected "the Union of these States, would not, and should not, survive the event."

The heavy Republican vote and its sectional character were almost as alarming as victory might have been. "Looking at the almost unanimous decision of the non-slaveholding States in favor of Frémont and at the tremendous majorities in some of them," wrote a Georgia editor, "the conviction is forced on us that popular sentiment in the North in reference to Southern rights is hopelessly diseased, and the

53

downfall of this grand and powerful Confederacy of States almost inevitable." A once conservative New Orleans editor confessed that " the settled convictions of a lifetime " had received a stunning shock. Almost as a mass the Northern states had voted for a candidate, the carrying out of whose principles would " inflict immeasurable degradation " upon the Southern people, reduce them to the level of serfs, deprive them of equality, and strip them of respect at home and abroad. Up to now he had laughed at anyone who suggested even the possibility of disunion. Now he had no laughter to offer in answer to the disunion pronouncements of his more impulsive neighbors. " Our enemies," he wrote, " for they are our countrymen only in name—are already laying their plans for the conduct of the next Presidential campaign . . . . Their program may be summed up in three sentences: Hatred of the South, desire to destroy the South, fierce and inextinguishable wish to bring immedicable ruin upon the South."

These two editors, one a Democrat, the other a Whig, revealed what was nearly the unanimous sentiment of the Southern press. Both were moderate, and neither accepted the more extreme demands of the Richmond *Enquirer* or the Charleston *Mercury*. Both saw the triumph of the Republican party as certain within the immediate future. Both bitterly resented the moral assumptions in the Republican advance and the degradation implied for the South Both understood that they faced the threat of social-economic revolution. They agreed with Thomas Clingman that the object of the Republican party was " the total abolition of slavery, the raising of the negroes to equality with us, and the amalgamation of the white and black races." Or as another put it, to allow the Republicans to secure control of the army, the navy, and the national treasury would mean " nothing but revolution, to be followed inevitably by the fiercest and bloodiest civil war known to history."

This was 1856. The next four years would not alter the attitude and feelings towards the Republican party. It would remain a threat. The shock and alarm, however, weakened after first days and contempt for the extremists of both North and South again found frequent expression. There was even more surprise expressed by Southerners at the violent reactions of the North to the Dred Scott decision than there had been at its excitement over the Kansas-Nebraska Act. In fact, the Court's decision attracted almost no comment from the Southern press. It was neither praised nor condemned. Instead, a rather surprising spirit of calm and moderation settled down over the South in contrast to the excited temper displayed by the Northern press. The great majority, with a sigh of relief, accepted the fact that Kansas would be free. They were weary of the whole business and ready with Parson Brownlow to "sink Kansas from the face of God's green earth after a third days notice." Talk of disunion, though more common than earlier, now met with equal assertions of loyalty to the Union and praise for its benefits. Even South Carolina seemed to have quieted down. "I never have known such a perfect calm in the public mind regarding the relations of the State with the General Government and Federal politics as now pervades it," wrote one of her citizens. ". . . she is fast becoming one of the most conservative Democratic States in the Union." Senator J. H. Hammond was advising her people to "avoid faction language & extremism." He believed that "999 in every 1000 voters" in the South would go "for the Union until it pinches them." As far as expressed public opinion was concerned, a Nashville editor seemed to speak for the great majority of the South when he said: "No more terrible calamity could befall the South than the rupture with the North . . . . Whoever would dissolve the Union and overthrow our present form of government, is the worst enemy the South could have."

This, however, was not a calm of surrender. It was rather the expression of the basically conservative attitude of a rural people now unusually prosperous. A Mobile, Alabama, editor put it in the form of a question: ". . . Will any sensible man undertake to tell us that the South can be aroused upon any existing issue with cotton at 13 cents, and negroes at $1,500, with lands rising in value, planters with pockets full of money, and merchants prospering? " He was certain from his knowledge of human nature and Southern politics that it could not be done.

He may have been right as far as existing material issues were concerned. But a Louisiana editor came nearer the truth when he insisted that Southern men had not forgotten the fact that they had been denied equality in national expansion, or that the Republicans had " abused and vilified us, exhausting the vocabulary of Billingsgate for epithets foul enough to designate us, proclaiming them from their hustings, their newspapers, and even their pulpits; [that] they have endorsed and set forth to all nations, as uttering their sentiments, the infamous production of one of their female writers, where we . . . are held up to the gaze of an eager world as slave-drivers, lost to humanity and accursed of God, driving the slave around the cotton field with thongs red in his own gore, like the veriest beasts of burden, when at last too old to be driven more, and useless, we are represented as, with cold-blooded and devilish barbarity, knocking out his brains."

It was to this widespread feeling of injustice, injured pride and moral degradation that the radical could always make his appeal. It was not so much

the actual fear that John Brown now inspired by his
raid on Harpers Ferry as it was the belief that Brown
had acted where others had only talked; that he had
the backing of respectable Northern leaders, and that
there was widespread Northern approval of his aims
if not his methods. The wave of anger which now
swept a united Southern people was far more the
product of Northern reactions to the raid than it was
to Brown himself.

The universal condemnation of John Brown, however, did not mean abject surrender of all to the forces
of disunion. It did mean that conservative men would
face the Presidential campaign of 1860 under a serious handicap. Most of their efforts would be consumed in checking a greatly strengthened radical
movement rather than in fighting the hated Republicans. They had lost the psychological advantage.
They were completely on the defensive. A Republican victory would mean defeat both at home and in
the nation. Those who held out would be left on
the sidelines, forced to choose between submission
and secession.

There is no sadder story in all American history
than that of the Southern conservatives in the final
crisis. They probably constituted a majority against
secession in the beginning but were too confused and

divided to gain control. Some were Democrats; many had been Whigs. Democrats were divided between Breckinridge and Douglas, and many former Whigs, after a trial with the Know-Nothings, had little enthusiasm for the new Constitutional Union effort. Under such circumstances, the advantage was all with the smaller group of determined, exasperated radicals who now talked loudly of Southern rights and Republican threats, and who were quietly, but not openly, planning secession. They arrogantly assumed that they alone stood for the honor, the interests, and the rights of the South. They hurled the charges of disloyalty, cowardice and weakness against all who would not join their ranks. They called them Abolitionists and Northern sympathizers. Instead of fighting the common enemy, conservatives were thus forced to spend their energies defending themselves, explaining their position, and asserting their loyalty to the South. They steadily lost ground and numbers, and what was more important, they lost confidence in their own cause as radical Republican campaign speeches came into print. Even fate was against them.

Nevertheless, a capable group of conservative editors in every Southern state held their ground, denounced disunion and exposed the hidden threat of secession in the Breckinridge movement. They kept insisting " that three-fourths of the adult population of the South have no desire for a dissolution of the

Union, but are willing . . . to live on terms of friendship with their Northern neighbors."

Lincoln's election, although generally expected, was a damaging blow. The long-discussed Republican danger to Southern institutions now seemed imminent. Emotions pushed reason aside and conservative men stood helpless while a comparatively small group of extremists shaped events. They could only plead for caution and delay. As the New Orleans *Bee* expressed it: "Moderate men—good men—men who have heretofore clung steadfastly to the Union, believed in its perpetuity, and discountenanced even a thought of dissolution, are now forced painfully, reluctantly, with sorrow and anguish, to the conclusion that it is wholly impossible . . . to tolerate tamely the present, or indulge the slightest hope of an improvement in the future." As the editor said: "The secession movement which [now] sprung up in Louisiana . . . grew too fast . . . to warrant the faintest hope of retarding its progress . . . . All that could be done by moderate, dispassionate, political and experienced men was to go with the current, endeavoring to subdue its boiling and seething energies . . . ."

Events in South Carolina and Lincoln's call for troops to crush resistance ended the last hope either of checking secession or of preventing civil war. The only choice now left to those who had held out to

the very end was either disgrace or joining in resistance. The bitterness and anger with which they made
their choice was so much a personal matter that it
can be revealed only through the individual. Yet
he spoke for the Southern masses who too had been
pushed into a war that few wanted and no one could
prevent.

It was a North Carolinian who bemoaned the fact
that he could now do nothing which his "judgment
and conscience" approved. "I cannot avert the war,
consistent with the re-establishment of a government
so good as that we pull down. Whilst I cannot hesi-
tate where no choice is left, only to fight for the South
and home, or for the North, if I should fall in such
a contest, I would find in a dying hour no comfort
in the conviction that I had sacrificed my life in a
just cause." Yet he was convinced that Lincoln was
either a fool or a devil and so urged his fellow citizens
to "fight like men for our firesides."

A South Carolinian spoke of his heart as rent by
the destruction of his country—"the dismemberment
of that great & glorious Union, cemented by the blood
of our fathers." "The American people seem de-
mented," he wrote. "They are exulting over the
destruction of the best and wisest form of government
ever sacrificed by God to man. Fools & wicked fools,
they know not what they do & may God forgive
them."

As the news of Georgia's secession flashed over the wires the most capable editor in the state sadly wrote: " To say that we *rejoice* at such an act would be simple hypocrisy—we cannot, and do not, rejoice. We have loved the Union with an affection pure and unselfish—not for any blessings it conferred, but because no pulsation of our heart has ever beat that was not loyal to the *great idea* of our ancestors— Union, Liberty and Fraternity.

" We have labored faithfully—God forgive us if it were unadvisedly—to preserve the Union. To it we clung with a devotion that knew no change and no shadow of turning; and, this hour we would as cheerfully as ever we lay down to childhood's slumber, lay down our life to preserve the Union, as our fathers made it, even for the short space of our children's lives . . . .

" That book is now closed . . . . Humbly [we] bow ourselves, not as slaves, but as free citizens, to the supreme decree of the State of Georgia . . . . Whatever the State requires of us shall be given to the utmost, cheerfully and obediently, to secure, maintain and defend forever against all mankind, the honor, the glory, the property and the happiness of this people."

And it was a soldier who believed that " in this enlightened age " there were few who would not acknowledge " that slavery as an institution " was " a moral and political evil," who, when news of military preparations reached him, wrote:

> The subject recalls my grief at the condition of our country. God alone can save us from our folly, selfishness & short sightedness . . . . I only see that a fearful calamity is upon us & fear that the country will have to pass through for its sins a fiery ordeal. I am unable to realize that our people will destroy a government inaugurated by the blood & wisdom of our patriot fathers, that has given us peace & prosperity at home, power & security abroad, & under which we have acquired a colossal strength unequalled in the history of mankind. I wish to live under no other government & there is no sacrifice I am not ready to make for the preservation of the Union save that of honour. If a disruption takes place, I shall go back in sorrow to my people & share the misery of my native state, & save in her defense there will be one soldier less in the world than now. I wish for no other flag than the " Star Spangled banner," & no other air than " Hail Columbia."

Then as war became a reality, he added:

> With all my devotion to the Union and the feeling of loyalty and duty of an American citizen, I have not been able to make up my mind to raise my hand against my relatives, my children, my home. I have, therefore, resigned my commission in the Army, and save in defense of my native State, with sincere hope that my poor services may never be needed, I hope I may never be called on to draw my sword.

The soldier was Robert E. Lee.

As to uniting the whole South on any measure of resistance worth a fig, the idea is absurd as it is unnecessary . . . . It is useless to talk about checking the North or dissolving the Union with unanimity and without division of the South . . . . The South must go through a trying ordeal before she will ever achieve her deliverance, and men having both nerve and self-sacrificing patriotism must head the movement and shape its course, controlling and compelling their inferior contemporaries.

—ROBERT BARNWELL RHETT

When a noble deed is done, who is likely to appreciate it? They who are noble themselves. I was not surprised that certain of my neighbors spoke of John Brown as an ordinary felon, for who are they? They have either much flesh, or much office, or much coarseness of some kind. They are not ethereal natures in any sense. The dark qualities predominate in them . . . . For the children of the light to contend with them is as if there should be a contest between eagles and owls.

—HENRY DAVID THOREAU

III: The Democratic Process
on Trial

To SINGLE OUT and assign relative importance to the varied factors that were involved in bringing on the American Civil War has always seemed to me a hopeless and useless undertaking. Political, social, psychological and economic forces were so confused and tangled together, and so many intangibles entered in, that clear-cut lines are seldom visible. And to make matters even more difficult, the struggle was as often over symbols as over concrete issues. At best, it is only possible to say with certainty that slavery, states' rights, and social-economic interests played a part, and somehow acted to produce an accumulation that made war inevitable—that is, if it was inevitable.

A far more important and far less difficult undertaking consists of asking and trying to answer the question as to how differences, which existed early and late, ultimately got into such shape that men in a democracy could not discuss them rationally, tolerate what could not be reconciled, or reach a workable compromise in regard to them. We know that there are some things men will not yield and for which they will give their lives rather than surrender. We also know that whole nations or regions have become involved in warfare by the acts and decisions of leaders who wrongly presumed to represent the feeling and desires of their people.

In dealing with the Civil War the important thing is to see how concrete issues, as they arose, came to represent abstract principles; and how conflicts between interests were simplified to those levels where men felt more than they reasoned and where surrender meant the loss of self-respect; where compromise was impossible because issues appeared in the form of right and wrong or involved the basic structure and values in a given society.

In such an approach, a correspondence which took place in November and December, 1860, between Abraham Lincoln, President-elect of the United States, and Alexander H. Stephens, soon to become vice-president of the Confederacy, is highly revealing. On November 14, Stephens had delivered one of the great speeches of his life before the legislature of Georgia. It was a Union speech. He had begged his fellow Southerners not to give up the ship; to wait for some violation of the Constitution before they attempted secession. Equality might yet be possible inside the Union. At least, the will of the whole people should be ascertained before any action was taken.

Abraham Lincoln, still unconvinced that there was

real danger, wrote Stephens as an old friend, for a revised copy of this speech. Stephens complied, and ended his letter with a warning about the great peril which threatened the country and with a reminder of the heavy responsibility now resting on the President-elect's shoulders. Lincoln answered with assurance that his administration would not either " *directly or indirectly,* interfere with the slaves, or with them about the slaves." " The South would be in no more danger in this respect, than it was in the days of Washington." He then closed with this significant statement: " I suppose, however, this does not meat [*sic*] the case—You think slavery is *right* and ought to be extended; while we think it is *wrong* and ought to be restricted—That I suppose is the rub. It certainly is the only substantial difference between us."

The reduction of " the only substantial difference " between North and South to a simple question of *right and wrong* is the important thing about Lincoln's statement. It revealed the extent to which the sectional controversy had, by 1860, been simplified and reduced to a conflict of principles in the minds of Northern people.

Stephens' answer to Lincoln was equally revealing. He assured Lincoln that he was not an enemy, and that *his* earnest desire, as he trusted was that of Lincoln also, was " to preserve and maintain the Union of the States," if it could be done " upon the principles and furtherance of the objects for which it was formed." This, however, he warned, could "never be attained by force." The people of the South did not fear that the incoming Republican administration would "attempt to interfere *directly* and *immediately* with slavery in the States," but what they objected to was that a subject, confessedly outside the Constitutional action of the government, had been made the central idea in the platform announced by the Republican party. This, said Stephens, was "simply and wantonly . . . to put the Institutions of nearly half the States under the ban of public opinion and national condemnation." It was this total disregard of the Constitution and the *rights* guaranteed under it, that produced Southern fears. It was the introduction into party politics of issues which projected action by Congress outside its Constitutional powers that had caused all the trouble. Men's private opinions regarding "African slavery" were not matters over which "the Government under the Constitution" had any control. Stephens used the word "Constitution" (or "Constitutional") seven times in his letter.

The significant thing in Stephens' reply is the reduction of sectional differences to the simple matter of maintaining Southern *rights* as guaranteed by the Constitution: the assumption that the Constitution even shielded slavery from criticism on moral grounds.

Stephens, too, was talking about a conflict of principles. He was assuming that the only " substantial difference " between North and South had to do with Constitutional *rights*. Thus he, with Lincoln, was revealing the fact that after years of strife the complex issues between the sections had, in the main, assumed the form of a conflict between *right* and *rights*.

This does not mean, of course, that these two leaders thought that all concrete issues, economic, social, and political, could be ignored. It simply meant that strife over concrete issues had revealed basic and fundamental differences in values and in men's understanding of the use to which institutions should be put: that back of their actions and reactions to concrete issues lay sharp differences in their understanding of what kind of a government we had established and what constituted the good society. It was these basic differences that cast their shadow over problems and interfered with rational discussion and possible compromises. So issues that might have yielded to the democratic process took on an abstract value and became part of an irrepressible conflict. Somehow nationalism, the abolition of slavery itself, and industrial capitalism were involved in every struggle.

The years from 1844 to 1850, which ultimately produced the Wilmot Proviso and the Compromise of 1850, form something of a watershed in the history of the democratic process in the United States. Before that period, there had been considerable creaking and jolting, but the undercurrent was strongly national and few seriously entertained the thought of disruption.

In the turmoil of growth and expansion in the period from 1815 to 1844, men seemed to realize the need for tolerance and a hospitality to ideas. States and regions grumbled and threatened when they could not have their way, but the possibility of yielding or compromising was always present where a swaggering pride in national growth and accomplishment widely existed. Somehow differences regarding tariffs, lands, roads and even banks were only occasionally made to symbolize wider sectional differences in regard to basic values. Individuals and states did sometimes make use of the moral or Constitutional appeal, but recruits were few and extreme action seldom went beyond talking and writing.

In the struggle over the admission of Missouri, Northern speakers in Congress denounced the " cruelty and immorality " of slavery, its "baneful consequences," and even its effects on fields and barns and fences. Mingled with the denunciation of slavery was a warning, echoed through the press, that the spread of slavery across the Mississippi would mark " the death-warrant of the political standing and influence of the free states," " their ' weight ' in national affairs," which, " if now lost " would be " lost forever." This idea of a power struggle also appeared in the effort to balance Missouri with Maine, and, to complicate matters still further, the issue of states' rights lay back of the arguments against placing restrictions on the institutions of a new state.

Yet in spite of harsh words and threats in the debates, Monroe was re-elected President without opposition in 1820, and the issues involved in the late struggle were quickly eclipsed by those raised in the administrations of John Quincy Adams and Andrew Jackson.

Nor did the ownership of slaves seem to do political damage in the decade which followed. John Taylor of Carolina, Nathaniel Macon and John Randolph, whom Arthur Schlesinger, Jr., says carried the democratic torch down to " the Age of Jackson," were all slaveholders. Jackson himself held slaves, as did his chief lieutenants, Thomas Hart Benton, Francis Preston Blair, and James K. Polk. The fathers of both Martin Van Buren and William H. Seward had a few slaves and neither son ever condemned his sire on those grounds.

In fact one might say that, in the 1820's, the fight against slavery, outside of Quaker ranks, centered in Virginia, Tennessee, and Kentucky, with liberal support from both North and South Carolinians. Criticism of the institution reached its height in the

Virginia legislature of 1832, where members questioned its economic benefits, pointed out its social dangers, and shamed its violation of human, Christian, and democratic values. James M'Dowell, Jr., went so far as to say: ". . . there is not a man in this body, not one, perhaps, that is even represented here, who would not have thanked the generations that have gone before us if, acting as public men, they had brought this bondage to a close." He warned that since slavery " contains an ingredient of political power in our Federal Councils, it will always be the subject of struggle—always defended by the most vigilant care and assailed by the most subtle counter-action. Slave-holding and non-slave-holding must necessarily constitute the characteristic feature of our country—must necessarily form the broad and indivisible interest upon which parties will combine; and does comprehend . . . the smothered and powerful, but, I trust, not the irresistible causes of future dismemberment." It was " for these reasons," he said, " that a crusade, in the name of liberty, but with the purpose of plunder, will be preached against the States that protect it,—they will be held up as the common enemies of man whom it will be a duty to overthrow and justice to despoil . . . ."

It is interesting to notice that there were few men in either the Missouri debates or in those of the legislatures who defended slavery in the abstract. As

Charles J. Faulkner said in the Virginia legislature: " Sir, I am gratified to perceive that no gentleman has yet risen in this hall, the avowed advocate of slavery. The day has gone by, when such a voice could be listened to with patience or even with forbearance."

Nor was the issue of nationalism versus states' rights one on which debate had been closed and sharp sectional lines drawn. The rechartering of the National Bank, the passing of protective tariffs and, particularly, the sweeping Court decisions of John Marshall had aroused the fears and driven the pen of John Taylor of Caroline. With profound understanding of what all this meant for those who tilled the soil, he made use both of history and theory to show that this was a confederation of sovereign states and not a consolidated union.

In 1827, when South Carolinians were ascribing all their economic ills to the passage of protective tariff acts, Robert J. Turnbull insisted that the one subject which should claim the attention of her citizens was " the tendency . . . toward a firm consolidated government." He paid scant attention either to history or to theory. He simply accepted the cold fact that the North and West had economic interests which called for a consolidated government such as the Fathers and the Constitution never intended. He saw economic ruin for the agricultural South fol-

73

lowed by a war on slavery. Hope, he thought, lay alone in the right and strength of the state to resist.

Yet while Virginians and Carolinians grumbled, John Marshall of Richmond in Virginia went on asserting the national character of our political system, and soon, Andrew Jackson of South Carolina and Tennessee would go the whole way and threaten the state of South Carolina with military subjection.

It was Jackson's threat to use force against a state that completed the transformation of John C. Calhoun from a nationalist to the defender of Southern rights. With the best disciplined mind of his generation and a logic unmatched inside or outside of Congress, Calhoun spent the mature years of his life trying to convince his stubborn fellows that ours was a federal Union—" a Union of States " which retained their sovereignty and all powers not specifically delegated away. He insisted that the government was " bound so to exercise its powers, as to give, as far as may be practicable, increased stability and security to the domestic institutions of the States "—which, of course, included slavery. This being the case, he warned " that no change of opinion or feeling, on the part of other States of the Union in relation to [slavery]," could " justify open and systematic attacks " thereon by them or their citizens, or any attempt to bar slavery from new territories or states " under the pretext that [it was] immoral, or sinful, or otherwise obnoxious."

This was in December, 1837. Calhoun was demanding for the South all that it would ever ask as a condition for remaining quietly within the Union. Yet Calhoun's efforts met with scant response from those he attempted to serve. " More vague and general abstractions could hardly have been brought forward," said John Jordan Crittenden of Kentucky. His resolutions, said Thomas Hart Benton, were " abstractions leading to no results." Howell Cobb, of Georgia, called him " an old reprobate " whose removal by " the Heavenly Father " would constitute " a national blessing."

There were many, even in South Carolina, who viewed Calhoun's passing in 1850 " as fortunate for the country " and as " the interposition of God " for its salvation. *The Works of John C. Calhoun*, published after his death by order of the legislature and distributed in large numbers to every section of the state, lay on the shelves unsold, and in three successive sessions of the legislature the proposals to erect a monument to his honor were defeated. The grim old Carolinian, who had dedicated his efforts to states' rights and the defense of slavery, had been right when he sadly concluded that " It was, perhaps, his misfortune to look too much to the future, and to move against dangers at too great a distance."

The swift changes which came in the 1840's to upset the balance which had kept the democratic process working in the earlier period, can only be touched in brief outline. It was a period in which steam, applied to transportation on land and water and to manufactures, wrought its miracles on space and interdependence; when industrial capitalism came to dominance in the North, and when cotton gave its people a confidence such as only a " King " could inspire. It saw a foreign war fought and won, a vast southwestern empire acquired, and the nation's boundaries pushed to the Pacific.

Yet success often brought disaster in its wake. Expansion offended many, gave the slavery issue a new twist, turned over the drive against the institution largely to the politicians, and made it the important distinguishing difference between North and South. It played havoc with the political parties, pushed the old Jacksonians aside, and set both Democrats and Whigs on the road to ultimate division and ruin. It created new third parties with enough drawing power to influence national elections, and brought forward a new breed of political spokesmen who were more interested in propaganda and reform than in making the democratic process work.

Equally important, this decade brought to an end that era of questioning and tolerance of ideas and replaced it with one in which men had all the answers and would neither tolerate differences nor yield ground. The Compromise of 1850 would be the last. After that, wheat and railroads, resentments and values, would unite the Northwest with the spreading industrialism of the Northeast into a workable unity moving into the Modern World of nationalism, freedom and "progress," while cotton, values, .and the need for justification and defense would shape the South into "a conscious minority."

The decade of the 1850's would, as a result, be one in which immediate differences would, perhaps unconsciously, be viewed as part of the basic conflict between values. Realities would be distorted and replaced by abstractions. Issues would seldom be faced on their own merits but would produce reactions determined by the implicit assumptions men were making about the nature of government, the right or wrong of slavery, and the rights of men or states under the Constitution. Calhoun had fixed the Southern assumptions in terms of sovereign states in a federation and the positive good of slavery; William H. Seward had stated the Northern assumptions in terms of a consolidated nation of people, the condemnation of slavery to the Dark Ages, and the moral law that was higher than the Constitution. The decade that began with the naive assumption that a compromise could bring peace and understanding was, therefore, to be one in which reactions would have little relationship to the realities, and each event would only confirm accepted opinions.

Fittingly, the first awakening jolt was produced by a work of fiction. From the pages of *Uncle Tom's Cabin*, written by a woman who, by her own confession, knew little of slavery as a reality, Northern men and women secured a " made-to-order " picture of slavery that required moral decisions and ultimate action. They would find it increasingly difficult to tolerate its continued existence on American soil. A fictitious Negro, Uncle Tom, and a fictitious white man, Simon Legree, would take the place of all Southern reality.

They were soon followed by an equally fictitious Stephen A. Douglas and his fictitious Kansas-Nebraska Act—fictitious because the real Douglas and the real Act were quickly replaced by what the interests and moral assumptions of the sections required. So convinced were Northern men of the existence of an aggressive " Slave Power " bent on spreading slavery throughout the nation, that they readily accepted the charges made in the so-called " Appeal of the Independent Democrats to the People of the United States." The " Appeal " was pure fiction and the storm it raised was without justification. Its authors were not Democrats, and the statement that " the freedom of our institutions " and " the permanency of our Union " were endangered, was as false as the charge that "the whole country" was about to be subjugated "to the yoke of a slaveholding despotism." There was not then, nor at any time thereafter, the slightest possibility that even Kansas would become a slave state. Douglas himself, speaking of the "vast territory, stretching from the Mississippi to the Pacific," had said that it was large enough "to form at least seventeen new free states" and that he was "safe in assuming that each of these [would] be free Territories and free States, whether Congress [should] prohibit slavery or not."

It is perfectly clear that whatever may have been Douglas' motives for introducing his Kansas-Nebraska bill, they did not include benefiting the South by the extension of slavery. And what is equally clear is that the South, as "a conscious aggressor," had not asked for this Act or for the repeal of the Missouri Compromise which it ultimately contained. Nor was Douglas a "slaveholder" about ready to move to Alabama, a "swindler" willing to barter his soul for the Presidency.

Yet the whole North raged in anger at the effort of "*the South*" to "extend its hell-born tyranny" and to give "to the Monster . . . the fairest land on earth." And the South, with as little regard for truth and fact, was soon insisting that unless Kansas became a slave territory she would not receive justice, and the Union was worthless. One historian has called it all "a tempest in a teapot." Another has insisted that in the whole Kansas struggle, the North was contending for what it already had, and the South for something it could not have used if it had gotten it.

It is not necessary to say that the facts in regard to "Bleeding Kansas" and the assault on Charles Sumner by Preston Brooks had scant relationship to the reactions which followed in both North and South. In Kansas, it is absolutely impossible to say how much that happened had to do with frontier conditions, land troubles, horse stealing, the influence of Missouri, and a half dozen other normal and abnormal matters, and how much they had to do with the struggle between freedom and slavery. Professor James Malin is probably right when he says that "the business of stealing horses under the cloak of fighting for freedom and running them off to the Nebraska-Iowa border for sale" is a neglected aspect of the struggle for "Bleeding Kansas."

Nor is it any easier to untangle the facts from the fiction which immediately transformed the foolish act of a South Carolinian against a rather foolish man from Massachusetts, into a demonstration of the effects of slavery on Southern character or, on the other hand, as an act provoked by the lies and abuses normal to antislavery men. Even these distortions would have been impossible had the Northern public not been willing to believe the false reports that

Brooks was armed, not only with a gutta-percha cane, but with daggers and pistols and an intent to commit murder with unanimous Southern approval; and had Southerners, for their part, understood that only a small percentage of Northern people approved either of Sumner, the man, or his extravagant words.

Yet the fact remains that Brooks's real intentions and the extent of Sumner's injuries are unimportant to history as compared to the fiction that added its part to the growing inability of men to make the democratic process solve their problems.

What becomes clear in a closer study of these tragic events, where reactions did not seem to fit the facts, is that men's reactions, after all, were born of something deeper than immediate events. On both sides of the Mason-Dixon line men were both vaguely and sharply aware of a conflict of values. The abstractions that had to do with every phase of national life, past, present, and future, were riding in the balance. The whole Modern World was pressing in upon them and vital decisions could not long be delayed. It was this which made for impatience, and which created a belief that what was done had some- how to do with national manifest destiny. Ends began to justify means, and the confusion reached its height in the John Brown raid.

That raid was in fact nothing more than the efforts of an irresponsible band of armed outlaws. It was childlike in conception and execution and bore the marks of insane leadership. Yet its purpose was a serious one which touched widely held Northern opinions and highly sensitive Southern interests. The raid itself can be dismissed as a minor, local affair; its effects were of momentous national import. Northern reactions were divided and conflicting, but underneath the general rejection of the means used, there was a vague and sometimes open approval of the ends sought.

The fact that six of the most prominent citizens of the Northeast had provided Brown with funds and knew his plans in general if not in detail, is of profound significance. Clergymen such as Theodore Parker and Thomas Wentworth Higginson; teachers such as Samuel Gridley Howe and Franklin B. Sanborn; and wealthy citizens such as George L. Stearns and Gerrit Smith certainly spoke for many besides themselves. The Boston *Post* commented without shame to the effect that if Brown were a lunatic, then one-fourth of the people of Massachusetts and three-fourths of her clergy were insane. It was only saying that there was something insane about hating slavery and yet permitting it to remain a recognized American institution. John Brown alone had found the solution. So the Reverend J. M. Manning of the Old South Church in Boston could speak of Harpers Ferry as " unlawful, foolhardy, a suicidal act," but

add, " I stand before it wondering and adoring," and
Horace Greeley could call it " The work of a mad
man," for the " grandeur and nobility " of which
he was " reverently grateful." Wendell Phillips came
nearer understanding the difficulty when he said:
" John Brown is the impersonation of God's order and
God's law, moulding a better future, and setting for
it an example." The abstraction had displaced the
fact. The day was dawning when " God's order and
law " as an end would justify the use of force and
bloodshed to achieve it.

In the South the widespread apathy which had
more or less characterized public opinion since the
1850 Compromise now quickly passed. Brown himself was forgotten, and attention centered on Seward
and other Republicans who had preached " the
higher law " which Brown had had the courage to
apply. The whole section which had tolerated the
Abolitionists was guilty. The South must unite and
resist. The British consul in Charleston spoke of
" the present state of affairs in the Southern country
as a reign of terror." The atmosphere of tension, born
of being a conscious minority under moral condemnation because of slavery, and the growing fears of slave
uprisings, broke into violence. Suspected persons
were treated to " tar and feathers " and driven out
of the country. The charge of inferiority was turned
into an assertion of superiority. Slavery became the

cornerstone of a finer civilization in which all the abstract values, ancient and modern, were to be preserved.

To such a situation the democratic process had no contribution to make. The struggle was between things for which men give their lives; things which they cannot discuss in a quiet reasonable way and which they cannot compromise. When radical Southerners were thinking only of secession, the line had been passed. When Thoreau could compare the execution of Brown for his efforts to stir a slave insurrection, to the crucifixion of Christ, and call him " the bravest and humanest man in all the country," and Emerson could speak of Brown making " the gallows as glorious as the Cross," the Northern intellectual, at least, had reached the point where only abstractions and ends counted. It might take considerably more jolting to remove the " Constitutional reverence " from the path of such middle-of-the-road men as Abraham Lincoln, but he too was bound to find, in time, the necessary excuses for throwing aside the old, hampering factors that kept the United States out of the Modern World.*

---

* The question of abstract values, and that of ends justifying means, lie at the heart of much of the controversy among historians regarding the Civil War. Because the Union was saved and slavery abolished through war, some critics have charged those who view the war as a national tragedy and who have tried to see both sides

That, of course, lay in the future. For the immediate present the problem was one of conducting a national election in the atmosphere created by John Brown against the background of the Kansas-Nebraska Act. The Republican party had emerged ostensibly to combat the supposed threat being made to spread slavery throughout the territories. It grew on the nourishment provided by "Bleeding Kansas," the attack on Sumner, and the "treachery" of the Supreme Court in the Dred Scott decision. Yet none of these things actually aided or were intended to aid the spread of slavery. As an Illinois man wrote in 1858: "Now I do not think that any sane man on earth thinks that all the presidents and all the coherents and all the Congresses, and all the Supreme Courts and all the slaveholders on earth, with all the Constitutions which could be drawn, can ever make Kansas a slave State." The real reason for

of the quarrel, with ignoring the moral issues involved and with believing that it was a "needless" affair. Such critics, themselves, are confusing ends and means and are assuming that war is an essential part of the democratic process. If their point of view is correct, then they must approve of John Brown and his methods; of Charles Sumner's speech on Kansas; and of all the other blunderings which made war inevitable. They also ignore the fact that most of the so-called causes of the war were themselves the result of the great changes which the forces creating the Modern World had wrought largely in the years after 1830. It was these forces that made long existing problems acute and clothed them with emotion.

Northern excitement lay deeper in the conviction that slavery itself was a morally offensive thing and was the basis for Southern opposition to the legislation demanded by the Northern people on their road to " progress."

The reason why the Southern people now demanded Congressional protection for slavery in the territories, of which there were none in which slavery could possibly have a chance, was nothing more than offended pride, a feeling of hopelessness in the race for equality, and an artificially created notion of strength in cotton and superiority in social values. They were not interested in accepting colonial status in the modern world of steam and organized capital. As a permanent minority, they saw a social-economic revolution impending.

Yet the immediate emotional drives which split the Democratic party and which carried the Republican party to victory centered about Stephen A. Douglas and his program for the territories. Not until the election was over and war was a reality did men discover that the issues which the fighting would ultimately settle had to do with nationalism, the abolition of slavery, government of the people, by the people, for the people, and those things which had to do with economic progress in terms of homesteads, railroads, banking, and tariffs. It was then they discovered that force as a means justified many strange ends. Yet they could still say as did Thomas Jefferson on another occasion:

> We feel that we are acting under obligations not confined to the limits of our own society. It is impossible not to be sensible that we are acting for all mankind.

. . . There is a feud between the North and the South which may be smothered but never overcome. They are at issue upon principles as dear and lasting as life itself. Reason as we may, or humbug as we choose, there is no denying the fact that the institutions of the South are the cause of this sectional controversy, and never until these institutions are destroyed, or there is an end to the opposition of the North to their existence, can there be any lasting and genuine settlement between the parties. We may purchase, as we have done in this instance [the Compromise of 1850], a temporary exemption from wrong . . . but there is no peace . . . .

—COLUMBUS (GA.) SENTINEL, Jan. 23, 1851

IV: The First Cold War

EACH NATION is important to its own people. Some nations, however, occupy a peculiar place in the history of mankind because of the contribution they have made to civilization as a whole. The United States, "conceived in liberty and dedicated to the proposition that all men are created equal," has always thought of itself as earth's great experiment in democracy, and others have generally accepted that estimate.

Back in the 1830's young Alexis de Toqueville confessed that "in America he saw more than America." As he put it: "I sought the image of democracy itself, with its inclinations, its character, its prejudices, and its passions, in order to learn what we have to fear or to hope from its progress." Sixty years later, Lord Bryce still viewed the United States as "an experiment in the rule of the multitude tried on a scale unprecedently vast, the results of which everyone is concerned to watch." Yet, he added, "they are something more than an experiment, for they are believed to disclose and display the type of institutions towards which, as by a law of fate, the rest of mankind are forced to move, some with swifter, others with slower, but all with unresting feet."

Consciousness of its democratic mission has been a part of the American story from the day when Thomas Jefferson penned the Declaration of Independence to that in the twentieth century when the United States threw its " moral and physical force into the scales of European republicanism," once to help make the world " safe for democracy," and once to advance the " four freedoms."

Yet in less than three generations after Jefferson had written his immortal document, the democratic process in the United States hopelessly failed. Men ceased to discuss their problems in a rational manner, refused to tolerate differences, rejected compromise, and defied the will of the majority. Then for four long, bitter, bloody years the armies of one group of Americans battled against the forces of the other until one was victor and the other lay in ruin and helpless defeat.

There had been physical and social differences in various corners of the United States from the beginning, but these had not prevented the realization of need for union. There had been issues before the Congress on which there had been sharp disagreement and sometimes harsh words. Yet, in spite of considerable grumbling, compromise or yielding had always been possible. When, however, issues began to involve the matter of right or wrong, of honor and self respect, of equality and rights, then compromise or yielding, or even rational discussion of issues, was no longer possible. To hold to one's position was a matter of principle—something to fight for or even to die for.

The historian's problem is, therefore, as has been said, largely one of trying to find out *how* and *why* issues increasingly tended to get into such abstract shapes that they could not yield to the democratic process; why " right " and " rights " crowded everything else aside. If he accepts Lincoln's statement that the government resorted to the use of force only to save the Union, and the Southern insistence that resort to secession was necessary for the protection of their domestic institutions [primarily slavery] then the historian must conclude that the elevation of nationalism to a supreme value on the part of the North, and of slavery to an equal value on the part of the South was the work of a single generation. An intense love of the Union and a willingness to accept its acts had not characterized all of the North in the days of the embargo and the War of 1812. The Hartford Convention of 1815 was not exactly an expression of good will towards sister states or the rule of the majority. As an English writer has said: " The mind of New England in this critical period . . . baffles inquiry." Nor, on the other hand, could one charge a section with knowing loyalty only to the state, which gave a Washington, a Jefferson, a Madison, a Monroe, a John Marshall, an Andrew Jackson, and a James K. Polk to the cause of nation building.

The historian must also remember that the harshest attacks on slavery in the 1820's and early 1830's were launched by Virginians, North and South Carolinians, the men of Tennessee and Kentucky. Everything the most rabid Northern Abolitionist would later charge against the institution was charged in the legislative halls of these states, and backed by antislavery societies, most of which at that time existed in these same states. Slavery, it should be remembered, had existed in the Southern states for over two hundred years without becoming a heavy burden on many Northern consciences. That too was a recent development.

Something indeed must have happened between 1830 and 1860 which strangely altered the patterns of American thought, pulled North and South apart and instituted a cold war between them. The period is highly complex and one can hardly hope to explain all that happened or played a part in producing a nation's tragedy. Yet a brief look at some of the forces at work in that period may give a few clues, and may serve, as the late Charles A. Beard once said, as " a damn dim candle over a damn dark abyss."

In the decades preceding the Civil War, two great forces were fundamentally altering the lives of men everywhere around the Atlantic Basin. The first of these, the Industrial Revolution, had already brought to much of western Europe the factory, mass production, world markets, and the concentration of capital for economic effort. It had spread to the northeastern corner of the United States and had turned the South into a great cotton field. What we think of as the Modern World was rapidly being created.

The material changes wrought by the Industrial Revolution everywhere require no comment. The term itself is enough to suggest them. But, for our purposes, one profound social change needs emphasis: *The total effect of the Industrial Revolution was vastly to increase the interlocking of human interests and the dependence of man on man.*

With the factory, labor became dependent on capital even for the right to work; capital, in turn, became dependent on machines and the labor to man them. Both became dependent on the producers of the raw materials that went into their product, and on the markets which consumed their mass production. Cities grew with industry, but no city could feed itself or consume the goods which its industries produced. They became increasingly dependent on the rural areas for food and most of the other necessities of life. Without widespread markets, they would have perished. Nations which became thoroughly industrialized, as did England by 1845, abandoned

93

their tariffs on foodstuffs, and reached out all over the world for markets and raw materials. Mankind was being bound together and made interdependent as never before in all the history of the world. The call for centralized political efficiency in the form of nationalism had never been so loud. No other force had ever worked so insistently to link the interest of individuals in different nations and within nations themselves so closely together.

In the United States the growth of interdependence was as marked as elsewhere. New England textile mills each year took a larger percentage of the Southern cotton crop. In return, the South increasingly depended on the North for its plantation supplies. By the 1850's, speakers often referred to New York City as " the prolongation of the South," and in late June and early July her hotels were filled with Southern merchants and planters, and her newspapers with advertisements addressed to Southerners. They had come for their annual supply of dry goods, hardware, boots and shoes, and other merchandise. J. P. Marshall and Company, Rogers and Company, and Phelps-Dodge and Company had branch houses in New Orleans; some, like Trenholm Brothers, had branches in Charleston, while others, like Daniel Parish and Company, had branches in five different Southern cities.

The planting of the cotton crop was financed by

advances made by Northern firms, and paid for at harvest with drafts on New York banks. It was shipped in Northern vessels, insured by Northern companies, and handled by Northern factors. In fact, as Professor Foner says, " Down to the outbreak of the Civil War, New York dominated every single phase of the cotton trade from plantation to market."

Meanwhile the farmers of the Northwest sent enormous quantities of corn, salt pork, flour, and whiskey down the rivers to Southern plantations, and the market gardeners of Virginia, each night, loaded their ships with potatoes, cabbages, fresh vegetables, and berries, according to the season, for the morning markets in Philadelphia, New York, and Boston.

In spite of surface differences, and all that historians have said, the most glaring reality of the day was interdependence—the uncomfortable fact that, in an economic sense, this was a single nation—" One World."

The second force, working towards the same end as the first, was the application of steam and electricity to communication. The first gave the railway, the steamship, and the power press. The second gave the telegraph. The effect of both was to cut space and to bring men closer together. Where up until now the vast spaces of the earth had been conquered by following waterways—the oceans between continents, and the lakes and rivers through continents—the railroad could penetrate great land masses and go wherever human needs dictated. Where before space was covered by the force of wind or animal and human exertion, now the tireless machine took over and began the task of shrinking the nations into convenient size.

The telegraph brought men, separated by great distances, within a few seconds of each other, and the power press made possible the creation and spread of common ideas from continent to continent, and from one end of a given nation to the other. Dr. Channing has even argued that " Modern life in all its branches from day to day, in peace and war, depends on the mobility of men and of things."

The United States, with greater spaces to be covered than any nation save Russia, made the most of these forces in the decade before the Civil War. Railroad building became a veritable passion as states vied with each other in the piling up of debts. Most of the mileage ran from east to west, but North and South were also joined along the eastern seaboard and from the Gulf to the Great Lakes. Other lines were projected or under construction by 1860 that would have cut diagonally from Charleston to Cincinnati and from Pensacola to New York. The telegraph followed the railway lines, and publishing for national consumption was a reality well before the outbreak of war.

How dependent the sections had become upon each other as producers and markets was strikingly expressed by a speaker at a Southern commercial convention in 1855. In a plea for greater home production, he declared: "From the rattle with which the nurse tickles the ear of the child born in the South to the shroud which covers the cold form of the dead, everything comes from the North. We rise from between sheets made in Northern looms, and pillows of Northern feathers, to wash in basins made in the North, dry our beards on Northern towels, and dress ourselves in garments woven in Northern looms; we eat from Northern plates and dishes; our rooms are swept with Northern brooms, our gardens dug with Northern spades and our bread kneaded in trays or dishes of Northern wood or tin; and the very wood which feeds our fires is cut from Northern axes, helved with hickory brought from Connecticut and New York." The picture was balanced by the confident assertion that if the cotton supply were cut off from Northern factories or the Mississippi River closed, the economy of the North would fall in ruin.

Again we must insist that the most patent social-economic fact of the period from 1815 to 1860 was the bringing of men closer together and the increase of *interdependence* to the point where the peace and security of all depended on an equal increase of that humility and intelligence and patience which make the democratic process work. Tolerance of differences, rational discussion of problems, and compromise where possible, would be the price men would have to pay for continued peace. No people could insist that their pattern was the one which all must accept. No people, with any grasp on the basic physical-social facts of the age, could have accepted disunion as a rational step. The United States had become an indivisible unit.

Yet the irony in the situation was that, in these very years, two distinct and differing social-economic systems were evolving side by side in the United States. One was predominantly agricultural; in the other, commerce, industry, and finance were increasingly important. The one depended on free white labor; in the other, by 1860, there were nearly four million Negro slaves.

The Industrial Revolution had played a mean trick on the United States. It had set one part of the nation to producing cotton to feed the hungry machines of Europe and given it a swaggering prosperity such as few Americans had ever known. Yet the spread of cotton and the creation of a new Lower South had not upset old institutions or old values. It only meant the spread of an agriculture based on the continued employment of the plantation system and Negro slave labor. It had not undermined men's reliance on local and state government as Thomas

Jefferson and John Taylor of Caroline had said should be the case. It had not weakened the belief in a rural-agricultural way of life as the only sound foundation for democracy and as the producer of those qualities in men designated as " gentle." It had justified in their minds the continued holding of slaves as beneficial to the Negro, to the white man, and to society as a whole.

This, however, was not the whole story. The rapid expansion of an agricultural area for the production of the raw materials needed in industry meant an unbalanced interdependence in which the raw producer moved steadily towards a colonial status. The advantages in the Modern World were all with those who owned the factories and those who controlled finances and marketing. Old World developments had already shown that, and the American South would soon find it out.

And, while the Industrial Revolution was spreading cotton and slavery over the Lower South, it was, as we have seen, also altering another part of the nation —the Northeast—by building factories and factory towns where young girls came from the neighboring countryside to toil; creating great cities with their prosperous merchants and their restless working classes; and spurring on a westward-moving farm population whose families provided the laboring force.

It was a completely new order and way of life, to

99

which not a single existing institution, relationship, or old value applied. Every basic concept and value had to be re-examined. The thinking which had served a society dominated by shipping and agriculture did not meet the needs of the new industrial order. Manufacturers, who were forced to find their raw materials and their markets in all parts of the country, and the merchants and bankers, who marketed and financed both wheat and cotton, were bound to be nationalist in their outlook. And all of them would see the advantages in a strong and active central government to give aid both to industry and transportation. Their hostility to slavery, like that of the farmers of the Northwest, would increase with time and with their advance into the Modern Age.

Here, then, were two rapidly expanding sections whose ways had been strangely widened by the Industrial Revolution. Yet even in a shrinking, interdependent nation, their *economic differences* did not necessarily imply hostility. A region producing raw materials and one engaged in industry may be complements as well as rivals. *Slavery*, however, was a different matter. It represented two entirely different understandings of the demands of Christianity, of democracy, and of progress. It had to do with things which cannot be compromised. It was not only an integral part of Southern social and economic life, but what was far more important, it symbolized the fact that South and North were moving in absolutely opposite directions. The one was holding firmly to the values of the past; the other was rushing madly into the Modern World.

Now the tragedy in this situation lay in the fact that, in the normal struggles for power in a government ruled by majorities, sectional interests became gradually tangled with basic differences and values. Conflicts were thereby lifted to the level of ideologies and civilizations. Men could compromise tariffs, internal improvements, and land programs; they must die for the preservation of their way of life, their ideals, and what they believed to be a civilization.

Said Professor Austin Phelps of Andover Theological Seminary: " Two opposing civilizations are in conflict here, and have been from the infancy of our Union." This was due, as Theodore Parker said, to the fact that " The South, in the main, had a very different origin from the North. I think few if any persons settled there for religion's sake; or for the sake of the freedom of the state. It was not a *moral idea* which sent men to Virginia, Georgia, or Carolina. ' Men do not gather grapes of thorns.' The difference in the seed will appear in the difference of the crop. In the character of the people of North, and South, it appears at this day . . . . Here, now, is the great cause of the difference in the material results, represented in towns and villages, by farms and factories, ships and shops. Here is the cause of differences in the schools and colleges, churches, and in literature; the cause of differences in men. The South with its despotic idea, dishonors labor, but wishes to compromise between its idleness and its appetite, and so kidnaps men to do its work."

The Charleston *Mercury* spoke for the South: "The North and South are two nations, made by their institutions, customs and habits of thought, as distinct as the English and French; and our annual meetings at Washington are not Congresses to discuss the common interests, but conventions, to contest antagonistic opinions and to proclaim mutual grievances and utter hostile threats." "No two nations on earth are, or ever were, more distinctly separated and hostile than we are," said Senator J. H. Hammond. "Not Carthage & Rome, England & France at any period." And when war came, the Reverend James H. Thornwell of South Carolina declared: "The parties in this conflict are not merely abolitionists and slaveholders; they are atheists, socialists, communists, red republicans, jacobins on the one side, and the friends of order and regulated freedom on the other. In one word, the world is the battleground, Christianity and atheism the combatants, and the progress of humanity, the stake."

Coexistence had evidently become a problem. Yet coexistence was rendered difficult if not impossible

by the assumption on the part of each that it represented the true American expression as envisaged
by the founding fathers and embodied in the Constitution. Neither thought of itself as struggling for
something new. Each was defending the old. Each
was innocent of wrong; each was confident of virtue.
Each firmly believed that the civilization which *it*
represented was not only the finest fruit of the
American experiment, but the pattern toward which
the whole civilized world would one day come.

Northerners were confident that they were in step
with progress. They pointed to their cities, their
factories, their commerce, their schools and their
literary output, and ascribed them all to the system
of free labor. Theirs was a land, as Wendell Phillips
boasted, where every man was the founder of his own
fortune; where families were trained up by the Bible;
where education lifted up not only the state but the
nation as well; and where industry used every drop
of water ten times over before it allowed it to fall
into the sea. Statistics were on the Northern side;
wealth and growth proved the case.

Then with more of vehemence than a desire for
accuracy, they pictured the South as they thought
it ought to be—backward, tumbledown, ignorant, and
immoral. Southern labor was starved and abused.
Without the incentive for personal gain, it was in-
efficient and discontented. Only by force and imposed

ignorance was the social-economic system maintained over its own people.

Southerners were just as confident of the superiority of *their* social-economic system. They praised the wholesome agricultural life where a man lived ten hours a day in the open air, rode his high-spirited horse as though he were part of it, followed the fox-hounds in spite of fences and ditches, brought down a partridge with each barrel, and, at the close of day, returned to a home " characterized by comfort without luxury, and simplicity without meanness." They boasted of its stability—of the absence of labor conflict, race riots, and wild-eyed " isms." Religion and politics were not mixed there; spirit rappings were not heard; women did not wear bloomers. A boy might go to college there and " never learn, or read a word in school or out of school, inconsistent with orthodox Christianity, pure morality, the right of property, the sacredness of marriage, the obligations of law, the duty of obedience to government." As George Fitz-hugh wrote: " Society has been so quiet and con-tented in the South,—it has suffered so little from crime or extreme poverty, that its attention has not been awakened to the revolutionary tumults, uproars, mendicity and crime of free society."

As to their much criticized labor system, they blunt-ly noted that its workers knew nothing of the ills of unemployment, neglect in time of sickness, and abandonment in old age. They insisted that the worker who always had a plenty of food, clothing, and shelter received a larger share of production than did the average worker elsewhere. Their condemnation of free society was expressed in their boasting. Like the communists and democrats of a later day, both assumed the perfection of their own system largely by pointing out the weaknesses in that of their opponents.

As stationary entities, these two civilizations might have lived together with only a minimum of friction, but in a world of shrinking space and increasing economic interdependence, a power struggle was inevitable. A clash of interests naturally suggested to each self-conscious civilization the desirability of allies, and the advantages of expansion. It was this effort to extend political power by the formation of alliances and the creation of satellites that produced a state of fear and tension which, in fact, amounted to a cold war between the sections.

It began when the South attempted to draw the young and growing Northwest into its orbit. That region had received the majority of its early population from the upland South, and its great river system had thrown trade in that direction. Building on these early advantages, Southern leaders, by concessions on lands and internal improvements, sought to develop these ties into a permanent political alliance. The famous Webster-Hayne debate was little more than a Southern bid for Western favor, and a Northern effort to counteract it. To the building of that alliance, John C. Calhoun gave as much attention as he did to the unification of the South itself, and on its foundations Stephen A. Douglas, of Illinois, built his political career. Its success gave the South control of the Democratic party, and made the Democratic party the dominant political power in the nation.

That was why the Northeast so bitterly opposed the next steps in expansion—the annexation of Texas and the war with Mexico. The whole business, it said, was a proslavery move, an effort to secure more territory for the expansion of a rival system. Joshua Giddings spoke of the conflict " between the interests of free labor and slave labor, between the Northern and Southern states," and declared that the admission of Texas would give " the balance of power " to the Southern states and thus enable them to " control the policy and destiny of the nation." Then with a magnificent tangling of material and spiritual values, he wanted to know whether the liberty-loving democrats of the North would be willing to give up their tariffs and their internal improvements in order to profit those who raised children for sale and dealt in the bodies of women.

Quickly the move to admit Texas as a state was

countered by a demand for the admission of Oregon. How much this had become a power struggle between hostile systems was shown by the assumption, widely made, that this was a kind of bargain between rivals— a balancing of interests. So when Texas was admitted and Oregon delayed, the cry of betrayal was loud and long. The North, said one, had been " politically bound, hand and foot, and surrendered to the rule and government of a slaveholding oligarchy."

Northern bitterness over the Mexican War was even more intense. Many viewed it as a war of aggression fought to "lug new slave states in." Senator Thomas Corwin, of Ohio, called it "wanton, unprovoked, unnecessary, and therefore, unjust." Charles Sumner referred to the American army as " a legalized band of brigands, marauders, and banditti [fighting] against the sanctions of civilization, justice, and humanity." He hoped it would be defeated and be forced "to pass submissively through the Claudine Forks of Mexican power,—to perish . . . like the legions of Varus."

The abrupt ending of the Mexican War and the acquiring of a vast new empire to the southwest only widened the terrain on which the cold war was being fought. The North made its move even before the war ended, to bar the extension of slavery from any territory acquired from Mexico. The South answered with threats of secession if denied equal rights in territory won by common blood. Tempers grew short, reasonableness even shorter. Congress became the meeting place of angry, defiant partisans. The press was given over to abuse and distortion. Each charged the other with aggression: Each insisted that its opponent was carrying forward a program of encirclement aimed at the ultimate destruction of its civilization. Vishinsky or Molotov or Dulles could not have conjured up a darker picture!

Fortunately, in 1850 such old master politicians as Henry Clay, Daniel Webster, Alexander H. Stephens, and Stephen A. Douglas were able to push abstractions aside and get back to the concrete problems of California, Texas, and fugitive slaves. They found that men could still deal with concrete problems in a rational way and that compromise was possible. They kept the democratic process working.

The larger result, however, was only to increase distrust, and to turn Congress, the only common meeting ground, into a place where more bitterness and hostility could be expressed. There, where " the windowless walls " shut out " all air, all light, all reality," personalities reacted to other personalities and speakers labored under the illusion that they expressed the emotions and attitudes of the masses far removed and quite unconscious of the irritations and excitement produced by personal contacts. Thus much that was artificial, immediate, and personal was translated into sectional hatred, and impressions given of the masses that had only to do with individuals. Political parties meanwhile splintered and went to pieces. The old Whig party died. Moves toward the creation of strictly sectional parties began to appear. Only the weakened and slowly disintegrating Democratic party made any pretense of being national in its appeal.

To save and bolster this last political prop of the democratic process, Stephen A. Douglas attempted to revive the old Northwest-Southern alliance. He would win the Northwest with internal improvements based on railroad building, and the South, by leaving the question of slavery in new territories to the settlers themselves. He succeeded only in revitalizing the cold war. Excited partisans accepted his proposal to leave the question of slavery to the settlers as an invitation to fight for control. " Come on, then, gentlemen of the slave states," cried William H. Seward. " I accept [your challenge] . . . in behalf of the cause of freedom. We will engage in competition for the virgin soil of Kansas, and God give the victory to the side which is stronger in numbers as it is in right." " We must send men to Kansas, ready . . . and able to meet abolitionism on its own issue, and with its own weapons," answered the Charleston *Mercury*. Like President Truman a century later in

Korea, or the Russians in Egypt or Syria, both were ready " to assist free peoples to work out their own destinies in their own way."

The frightening thing about the national situation in the next few years, as Kansas bled and political parties disintegrated, was the steady growth of distrust and fears and hatred. Social and intellectual contacts between North and South were sharply curtailed, and a kind of iron curtain hung between them. Every Northern traveller who crossed the Mason and Dixon line was viewed as a possible Abolitionist. Northern teachers and Northern pedlars were seized and driven out. Waves of panic swept the section as rumors of slave insurrections, stirred by outsiders, spread from neighborhood to neighborhood. Tar and feathers were applied indiscriminately, and suspicion was the same as conviction.

Then with equal zeal they turned on Northern books, periodicals and schools, and set about creating a Southern brand of each. Bitterly they denounced anyone who " preferred the trashy stuff of Boston, Cincinnati and New York, to the pure, healthful, home-made productions of Southern pens." In a few cases they actually engaged in " book burning." They called their sons home from Northern schools where, they charged, young men imbibed " doctrines subversive to all old doctrines." They asked that only native teachers " born to the manor " should be employed, and that they should be supplied with text-books which inspired faith in Southern institutions and inculcated Southern patriotism. They urged Southerners to boycott Northern summer resorts and to confine travel to places friendly to the South. They would, if you please, seal the Southern mind against outside influences and mold it to an acceptance of the superiority of all things Southern.

Witch hunting among their own people naturally followed. Persons with liberal opinions fell under suspicion. A few college professors lost their jobs; others chose to resign and cross the border to the north. One of them fired a parting shot that has a modern ring: "You may eliminate all the suspicious men from your institutions of learning, you may establish any number of new colleges which will relieve you of sending your sons to free institutions. But as long as people study, and read, and think among you, the absurdity of your system will be discovered and there will always be found some courageous intelligence to protest against your hateful tyranny." He was right, but the protests of the few did not save the section from that deadly intellectual miasma which comes from the irresponsible broadcasting of suspicion.

On the other side of this iron curtain it was not necessary to exercise caution. Few Northerners had ever read anything written in the South, and the works of Fitzhugh, Holmes, and Hughes were scarcely noticed. Few Northerners had traveled across the Mason-Dixon line, and the few who did, returned to give so dismal a picture that few cared to follow. The only slaves known to the North were runaways or a fictitious one by the name of Uncle Tom, who at least had a Cabin. Some did go to the trouble of burning the Constitution because it protected Southern interests, and there were a few cases of persecution for the defending of Southern ways. But on the whole men felt safe and confident that all was on their side.

With these developments, the idea of two civilizations locked in deadly conflict reached its climax. The struggle was now entirely on the high ground of principle. Each party thought of itself as struggling to preserve "the last best hope of mankind." Each was convinced that it stood on the defensive against unprincipled aggression. It was useless to argue with such people; it was impossible to reason. Armories began to be built, funds appropriated for arms and military companies organized. Strength alone could give protection.

But making onself strong did not, they said, mean war. The ability to use force was the surest guarantee of peace. "You have only to put the government in a position to make itself respected," said Senator Trumbull, "and it will command respect." Build up the nation's arms, urged the Chicago *Tribune*, and "thousands of bullies . . . [will] become as mild as so many sucking doves." "The national government may have to *show* its teeth," echoed the New York *Tribune*, "but it is not at all likely that it will have to *use* them." Sound preparation to use force was the best way to insure peace.

It was, therefore, inevitable in such an atmosphere that the extremist (perhaps we should call him the abstract idealist), should have appeared with his doctrine that the end justifies the necessary means. Bearing letters of marque from God, his patience exhausted by delay, he was ready to accept personal responsibility for a people's failure to meet their obligations to mankind. He was certain that the only language the opponent could understand was that of force. He was willing to risk war if that were the price for setting the world in order.

It seems strange that men who were convinced that the opposing civilization carried within itself the seeds of its own destruction should not have been willing to wait patiently for nature to do its work. Middle of the road men were playing for time to compromise. Seward was convinced that the Border States were, day by day, drawing away from the South and toward freedom. Fitzhugh was equally certain that the turmoil and strife inherent in a free society would soon destroy the whole edifice. "Towards slavery," he said,

" the North and all Western Europe are unconsciously marching."

But patience is not a characteristic of the extremist. Innocence and virtue excuse him from obedience to objectionable laws, and endow him with the privilege of righteous indignation. So when the democratic process ceased to function, and moderate men stood helpless before the mounting fears and hatred and anger of both sides, the Yanceys, the Rhetts, the Charles Sumners and the John Browns and their " fellow-travelers " had their chance. Their eyes had seen the glory of the coming of the Lord, and with their help He would trample out the vintage where the grapes of wrath were stored. Out in Kansas, on the floors of the Senate, at the party conventions, at Harpers Ferry, they translated the threats and challenges of a generation into action. They made war inevitable. They forced a nation to use the most undemocratic method known, in order to save the democratic values. They caused the defenders of one social-economic system to strike, with the air of righteous crusaders, for independent existence so that they might preserve what they believed was the only sound democratic order. They caused the defenders of the rival social-economic system to fight for four long bitter years for the preservation of a Union which was worth saving, said its great spokesman, because it represented earth's great experiment in government of the people, by the people, for the people.

And besides, said a spokesman for the new business interests: "We cannot afford to have established on this continent the intolerable restrictions to commercial intercourse, which are fast dying out among the nations of Europe."